Prais

Bad Be
People Problems and
Sticky Situations

"Gregg Ward hits the proverbial nail right on the head in this unique book. His no-nonsense, yet nice and easy style, together with his relevant, practical, real-life insights, make this an important "gotta read" book. He's clearly been there and done it, and his experience comes through on every page."

Mark Lutchen
Partner
PricewaterhouseCoopers LLP

"Too many business and management books submerge the reader in complex, unrealistic theories, but not *Bad Behavior, People Problems and Sticky Situations*. Ward has worked with thousands of people in hundreds of companies: he's truly seen it all. You'll find good, solid, real-world advice and tools in here."

Gary Dichtenberg
President
Professional Development Associates

"Practical and down to earth, Ward takes over where the theories leave off. This is how to cope in the real world."

Ann Hesselink, Esq.
VP, Mergers & Acquisitions
The Geneva Companies

"As an experienced manager I found treasure, wisdom and inspiration in Ward's book. I have always wanted to be an effective, motivating and successful leader – this book provides a great road map for building that legacy."

Sharon A. Winston
Regional Vice President
Lee Hecht Harrison

INDIE BOOKS
INTERNATIONAL

Bad Behavior, People Problems and Sticky Situations

A Toolbook for Managers and Team Leaders

By Gregg Ward

Indie Books International Oceanside, California USA

Indie Books International
2424 Vista Way, Ste 316
Oceanside, CA 92054
800-514-4467
indiebooksintl.com

Originally published 2002, 2004 by Winding Creek Press.

executive editor/director • donna orlando
research, design and marketing director • melody browne
layout and graphic design • john magee and allan manzano
assistant copy editor • stacie linardos
consulting editors • nancy crosby, phil dixon,
mark lutchen, mark schall

For 2014 Revised Edition:
Production Coordinator/Consulting Editor – Walter G. Meyer
Cover Redesign – David Maxine

Library of Congress Cataloging In Publication Data

Ward, Gregg, 1960-

Bad behavior, people problems and sticky situations: a
toolbook for managers and team leaders / by Gregg Ward –
revised from 2004 editon in 2014

Includes bibliographical references and index.

Library of Congress: 2014956337
ISBN 1941870-074

1. Interpersonal relations.   2. Supervision of employees.

3. Problem employees.   4. Conflict management.

5. Personnel management. I. Title.

Dedicated to every manager

and team leader

who is committed to

making a positive difference.

Publisher's Note

This book is designed to provide information in regard to the subject matter covered. It is sold with the understanding that the publisher and author are not engaged in rendering legal advice. If legal or other expert assistance is required, the services of a competent professional should be sought.

Every effort has been made to make this book as complete and accurate as possible. However laws, regulations, policies and procedures regarding harassment and discrimination, management's roles and responsibilities, and general management and human resources practices are constantly changing. Therefore this book should be used only as a general guide and not the ultimate or definitive source of information on the issues addressed within it.

The purpose of this book is to educate and entertain. The author, Winding Creek Press, and Indie Books International shall have neither liability nor responsibility to any person or entity with respect to loss or damage caused, or alleged to be caused, directly or indirectly by the use of any of the tools, techniques or information contained in this book.

Any person not wishing to be bound by the above may return this book to the publisher for a refund.

Acknowledgments

I had planned on my first book being a massive, thousand-page, reference volume on workplace diversity until my wife and some very reasonable colleagues and clients made it clear to me that the world didn't need such a book right now. Instead, they encouraged me to write an easy-to-use and engaging toolbook on interpersonal communication based on my experiences working with big and little companies, non-profits and government agencies. So, to all those people who convinced me to write this book instead of that heavy tome on diversity, thank you!

Individually, I want to acknowledge my wife, Donna Orlando, who is the most incredible life and business partner anyone could ever hope for. Her love, encouragement, thoughtfulness, wisdom, maturity, guidance and gentle cynicism are invaluable to me and to our families. When it comes to my writing and speaking engagements, I lovingly consider Donna my personal "crap detector," and she has been that and so much more on this project. Thank you Donna for making such a powerful contribution to me and to the lives of everyone you touch.

This book would never have been completed (I'm serious!) without the constant help, ideas, street smarts, badgering and hard labor of my researcher, personal assistant and marketing wizard, Melody Browne, who deserves much more credit than these job titles could ever offer. Thanks also to Peter Knapp for his sound advice and counsel on this project.

A heartfelt thank you to our champion and business advisor Mark Lutchen at PricewaterhouseCoopers, and to Phil Dixon of Colliers International, Arthur Matthews at Cornell University, Nancy Crosby at QUALCOMM, Carolyn Greene of AXA Financial Services, and Sharon Winston with Lee Hecht Harrison for your insightful and valuable feedback on my drafts and for offering those amazing comments quoted on the back and inside covers. By the way Phil, thank you for coining "F.A.C.T.," it's dead brilliant.

There are many terrific people from all walks of life who have generously contributed their time and expertise to my work over the last twenty years. I would like to acknowledge and thank them here: My consulting colleagues and dear friends Mark Alan Schall of Orlando-Ward & Associates in New York City, Michael Grant Hall of Orlando-Ward & Associates here in San Diego, and Gary ("Straight Talk") Dichtenberg of Professional Development Associates in Atlanta.

Also, thanks to Stewart Arnold, CEO of InetMedia, Long Island, NY; Dean Jim Curran and Dr. Ray Pitt at John Jay College of Criminal Justice; Dianne Dyer at The Titan Corporation; Arvind Garg, a good friend and brilliant photographer; life advisor Ann Hesselink, Esq.; Audrey Goodman and Beverly WInkler at Merck Medco; the colorful and inspirational Ron Johnson; Captain John Kohut and Kathey Bailey of SPAWAR PMW 101/159; Kathy Leach at PWC; Allan Manzano, one of the most talented graphic designers I've ever met; Cathy Mellinger at Colliers International; John Magee at Acorn Press; Tamara McLeod and Cathy Dellas at San Diego State University; Gary Rossi and Jeran Bining, two terrific management consultants here in San Diego; media guru Tony Schwartz in NYC; Terry Simmons and Peggy Hazard with Simmons Associates in New Hope, Pennsylvania; Mike Sullivan and Rich Paul of the employment law firm of Paul Plevin Sullivan LLP, San Diego; Teri Swanson of Lee Hecht Harrison, NY; Sir Christopher Warrick of London; the gang on Winding Creek Drive, and all of the Orlando-Ward & Associates actors around the world.

Lastly, if I didn't acknowledge the incredibly positive influence of my father, the writer/outdoorsman Gene Ward, and thank my wonderfully supportive mom Carol Ward, and my brothers Gene and Guy, and my incredible, amazing, brilliant son Leigh, I'd really never hear the end of it. Seriously, they all really deserve to be thanked because they have always been there for me, and have always believed in me and in my dreams. Thank you!

Gregg Ward

Bad Behavior, People Problems and Sticky Situations

A Toolbook for Managers and Team Leaders

By Gregg Ward

CONTENTS

CONTENTS, continued...

Introduction

About this new version: Times have clearly changed since this book was first published in 2002, and I've received both praise and feedback on it. Although the concepts and lessons still apply, it was time for me to update it to make it even more relevant for today's business environment.

Why this book? People kept asking me for it! I'm in the business of creating and facilitating interactive training programs on diversity, conflict, harassment, leadership, teamwork and change – the so-called "soft issues." I've been doing this kind of work since the mid-1980s. After almost every program a group of managers and supervisors will come up to me, tell me what a great facilitator I am (thank you!) and ask me if I have a "toolbook" that builds on the work they did with me. "We need a 'how to' manual," they say. "Something to pull off the shelf and use on-the-spot, without a lot of study or hassle."

Why do they want such a book? Well let's face it, when it comes to training on interpersonal skills, most MBA or corporate management programs fall a bit short of the mark. Sure they'll give you a lot of organizational theory, matrix, and cross-functional management gobbledy-gook – most of which we tend to forget the moment we leave the class-room. But when it comes to basic, everyday interpersonal interactions like talking and listening, responding to emotionalism, or handling bad behavior, people problems and sticky situations, many managers feel unprepared. They really want practical advice and help. So this is that how-to "toolbook" people keep asking me about.

What's In It? In the chapters at the beginning of the book, which I call the "Primers," I offer overviews on most of the big issues every manager needs to know about; i.e. managing and motivating people, workplace harassment, diversity and leadership. I've populated these chapters with stories taken from my own experiences working with and for many different kinds of organizations. Of course, the individual names and situations have been changed to protect the innocent...and the guilty.

The mid-section of *Bad Behavior, People Problems and Sticky Situations* is filled with basic, simple, clear and easy-to-use interpersonal management tools and techniques, most of which you can teach yourself to use in less than five minutes. The tools are laid out simply and clearly – so you can follow them step-by-step. In the last third of the book, you'll find a raft of realistic case studies – all based on actual problems my clients have faced – which you can use to develop and test your knowledge and skill.

In addition to reading the book through at least once, I'm also hoping you'll turn to it when you're facing specific bad behavior, people problems and sticky situations and wondering "What the heck do I do?!" To accommodate this use, I've arranged the book by challenge/problem and cross-referenced each one with tools to make using it that much easier. If you're in a real hurry, check the "Index by Problem."

Do The Tools Work? My clients tell me they do. Every tool in this book has been tested and tried many times in many different types of organizations, including big and small companies, city, county, state and federal government agencies, and non-profit organizations like health care groups, colleges and universities. Most people report back that the tools were simple, easy to use, and actually worked with a fairly high success rate.

Can I guarantee they'll work for you? Sorry I can't. Simply because people are human. Not everyone uses the tools exactly the same way, and not everyone responds to the tools in the same manner. However, in general, I've found if you use the tools as instructed after practicing them with a trusted colleague, the situation you're addressing will improve and/or be less stressful for everyone.

Will It Hurt? Well, that depends on your pain threshold! Seriously, there's no question that using most of these tools will require you to be clear, patient and occasionally blunt. If you're "risk" averse and/or you're constantly trying to avoid confrontations, then sure some of these tools – like "Straight Talk" – are going to be tough for you to use. But don't forget, if you're a manager, supervisor or team leader, sooner or later you're going to face some bad behavior, people problems and sticky situations that require your attention and action. These tools are designed to help get you through those situations as cleanly as possible.

What If I Need Help? It's always a good idea to ask for help or guidance from someone with experience before wading into any sticky situation. Again, I recommend you practice using these tools on a colleague before you use them in real life. When in doubt about anything, always talk to a human resources or legal professional about the problem before attempting to handle it yourself. They might take the problem off your hands or offer to let you practice using the tool on them. If you don't have an HR or legal person available to you, or one with whom you're comfortable, then work with a higher-level manager with lots of experience, people skills and street smarts. They've probably seen your problem before and can give you help and guidance.

If you get stuck, or have a specific question, or need coaching, e-mail me at gward@greggwardgroup.com, and I'll try my best to respond in 24 hours.

One Last Note. The United States is the most litigious society in the history of civilization. More people are suing each other, and their employers, for more things than ever before. As a manager or supervisor, whether you like it or not, your responsibility is greater than that of a line employee and sooner or later, you will be called upon to handle bad behavior, people problems, sticky situations and make tough decisions. The outcome of some of these problems could be challenged in court, with you sitting in a witness box or – even worse – at the defense table.

We strongly urge you to document, document, document everything you do. Whenever you get involved in handling bad behavior, people problems and/or sticky situations, make a note of the problem, the date and time, the people involved, what they said/did and what you said/did in response. In the event of a lawsuit, those notes may be your best protection.

Gregg Ward
San Diego CA
Spring 2014
gward@greggwardgroup.com

Primer One

Bad Behavior,
People Problems and
Sticky Situations...*Defined*

Bad Behavior. A few years ago, while doing a "pulse check" (internal focus groups and private interviews) for the leadership of a large corporation, I uncovered some bad behavior that shocked even me, and I thought I'd seen it all. After receiving anonymous tips from low level employees, it became clear to me that an executive in the company's administrative group, with the help of a few colleagues, had been secretly siphoning off hundreds of thousands of dollars every year from internal expense accounts. They'd been using the money to buy expensive cars, homes and boats for themselves and their families.

When a secret internal audit confirmed my findings, the CEO decided to dismiss the executive and his cadre in one fell swoop. But the company didn't want the group tipped off in advance as to their fate. So, the CEO asked an assistant to set up a run-of-the-mill budget meeting with the executive, to see if they could trim some fat.

On the appointed day, the CEO and a team of security agents flew into town to deliver the bad news and escort the group from the building. Without warning, the offenders were called together in a conference room, terminated on the spot, and asked to clean out their personal belongings from their offices.

Now here's the shocking part: Out of the desks and closets of these folks came automatic and semi-automatic rifles, 10-inch hunting knives and a host of handguns, pistols and other military-type weapons and ammunition! Remember, this was an administrative group – literal paper-pushers – and yet they were armed to the teeth! After pausing to push up their jaws, the CEO and his security team confiscated the weapons and ejected the group from the building. This bizarre little incident helped me to realize that no matter how much experience you have, it's never safe to assume you've seen it all.

The term "Bad Behavior" refers to all those behaviors that could get the person (or people) engaging in them "on the job" in trouble with your organization or the law. Many behaviors fall into this category, from offensive language or joke-telling to theft and property destruction.

Here's a partial list:

- Harassment (including creating a hostile work environment)
- Discrimination
- Violence and fighting
- Theft of company or personal property, funds
- Retaliation against people who don't accede to unreasonable or illegal requests
- Retaliation against whistle-blowers
- Substance abuse, distribution, dealing
- Violating city, state and federal employment, environmental, and trade laws
- Gambling, racketeering
- Surfing pornographic sites on the net using company equipment; downloading and/or e-mailing pornographic and other offensive material
- Bribery and kickbacks
- Provocative, foul and/or abusive language
- Sending "hate" mail and anonymous e-mail with threats and/or hate messages
- Obstructing criminal investigations
- Inappropriate/lewd dress
- Destruction of property, arson
- Spying and/or voyeurism
- Inappropriate use of company credit cards or funds
- Fraud
- Third party harassment (outsiders harassing your employees or vice versa)

If you become aware of any of these issues there are tools you could choose to use that should de-escalate the situation or put it "on hold" until trained professionals (such as police officers and attorneys) become involved.

But everyday, run-of-the-mill bad behavior like offensive, sexually charged language or inappropriate dress, is one thing. You, as the individual manager or supervisor, may (actually, I'll say "should") be able to handle problems like these on your own. However, really bad behavior, like physical assault, threats of violence, or extortion, is another matter entirely. Unless you're a cop or firefighter, you really shouldn't try to handle these kinds of behaviors single-handedly. You're not being paid to put yourself at risk of physical injury or death. You have the right to – and should – get the heck out of any dangerous workplace situation like this and go for help.

People Problems.   Recently, I was hired by an online training company to mediate between Chuck, a client service director, and Lauren, one of his team members. The two were having trouble communicating on just about everything, and according to Chuck, she was frequently rude to him, took an inordinate amount of time responding to his calls and emails, and regularly ignored him in team meetings. It had gotten to the point that Chuck – a quiet, caring guy whom most people liked and respected – had thrown up his hands in frustration and was thinking about terminating her.

In a private, pre-mediation meeting Chuck told me that for a long time, he'd felt completely powerless and ineffectual with Lauren, but he didn't want to fire her because she did her job well. She was a "good performer," he said, a self-starter whom the clients liked. I asked Chuck if he could point to any events or incidents that had occurred between them that might explain her behavior toward him. After some thought, he recalled that a year previously Lauren had come to him with an idea to expand the training services they were offering a particular client. She asked that she be allowed to personally lead the program development effort. Chuck thought it was a great idea, but the firm's head office wanted Chuck to contract a specialist, a woman named Althea who had a Ph.D. in distance learning, to develop the new service for this client. Contracting such a specialist would enable the firm to charge the client a higher rate and increase its revenue.

So Chuck did as he was told by his boss and contracted Althea to handle the development job. He broke the news to Lauren in private, explaining the head office's bottom-line logic in as caring and as sympathetic a manner as he could. As far as Chuck could tell, she took the news as well as could be expected. A few months later, he gave Lauren a higher-than-normal bonus, and thanked her publicly for bringing in the new business. He remembered that when he told her about the bonus, Lauren didn't seem particularly enthusiastic.

During my private meeting with Lauren, I waited for her to bring up this incident, but she said nothing. Instead, she spoke in general, emotional terms, saying that Chuck was ineffectual, a "wimp" of a manager, who didn't deserve her time or respect. She spent a lot of time denigrating Chuck, nit-picking on small events that had occurred over the years, and growing more and more angry as she did so.

Finally I asked her why she was so angry with Chuck. Sure enough, the contracting of the specialist was at the heart of it. But there was more to the story which Chuck had neglected to tell me about. According to Lauren shortly after the head office made their decision, Chuck announced that Althea would report directly to Lauren, Althea's junior in both age and experience. A few weeks later, Lauren discovered that Althea earned at least twice her hourly rate and that the client was being billed 50 percent above this rate!

Lauren was furious about the whole affair and admitted to me that she was actively searching for a job outside of the company because of it. She said she felt that Chuck and the company had taken advantage of her and insulted her to boot by having Althea report to her. I told Lauren that I certainly understood her feelings and her desire to leave. But I added that unless she told Chuck how she felt and exactly why she was leaving, she would carry the emotional baggage from this situation into every relationship with every manager she worked for in the future. I'm no psychologist and I don't honestly know if there was any psychological truth in what I was saying, but it seemed to make sense to Lauren, and she agreed that she would feel a lot better if she could just tell Chuck everything before she left.

During the mediation session with the two of them, I asked Chuck to discuss the incident and explain his decision to have the specialist report to Lauren. Chuck said that since the new service was her idea, he believed Lauren would be very flattered by having overall responsibility for the project, and be proud of the fact that she was supervising a top specialist. Of course Lauren didn't see it that way at all, and with tears in her eyes told Chuck how Althea had completely ignored and disrespected her and how "used, insulted and patronized" the whole situation made her feel. On top of this, Lauren was convinced Althea had done a "half-assed" job on the project and had repeatedly insulted the client by ignoring their requests.

Now, I had prepared Chuck in advance for what Lauren might say, but her words and level of emotion still devastated him. He asked her why she hadn't said anything about it before and she replied she was too embarrassed. She felt it would be "unprofessional" to complain. At this point, the light bulb went on for Chuck, and he nearly broke down as he made one of the most sincere and heartfelt apologies I've ever seen a manager offer a subordinate.

Then Lauren sincerely apologized to Chuck for being so rude and disrespectful to him and for not saying something to him in the first place. She said she really liked working for the company and wanted to stop her job search. Chuck, who'd had a hunch she was looking to leave, was delighted, and together they developed a strategy for putting their relationship back on track, upping her hourly rate, and giving her more responsibility for program development and recognition for her ideas and efforts.

Please don't misinterpret my reasons for telling you about Chuck and Lauren. I'm definitely not implying that every manager needs to know how to conduct a complex mediation like this, to bring two people together and resolve this kind of thorny people problem. (By the way, I used "The 60-minute Mediation" tool on page 69 although the process, given the complexity of the relationship and events, took much longer than 60 minutes.) But I am saying that managers need to be aware of how their decisions, actions and assumptions may impact the people on their teams. Bottom line, Chuck, as a manager, should have communicated his thoughts to Lauren throughout the process. And Lauren should have communicated hers to him.

If you are facing a difficult people problem like Chuck and Lauren's, I believe you need to be prepared to...

1. Ask the question, "What's bothering you?"
2. Manage the strong emotions that may come with the answer, and
3. Formulate a workable strategy for moving forward.

In general, the term "People Problems" refers to individual problems that employees have, or conflicts, disagreements, miscommunications and troublesome, destructive behaviors that occur between individuals and/or groups. These tend not to be explicitly prohibited by company policy, nor are illegal per se, but can be a big headache for the individuals and/or groups involved, not to mention their managers and the organization in general.

Again, this book provides you with some tools to help you to handle these things. But remember, all the tools in this book are optional. If you don't want to use them, you don't have to. If you feel uncomfortable handling a "people problem" on your own, contact someone – like an HR or legal professional, or a more experienced manager – and let him or her coach you through it.

On the next page you'll find a partial list of what I call "people problems."

● Gossip
● Affairs
● Lying
● Disparaging, disrespectful, belittling, degrading, abusive remarks or gestures
● Work stoppages/slowdowns
● Hiding/withholding information
● Subversive or undermining behavior or remarks
● Excessive after hours fraternization with subordinates
● Exclusive/prejudicial behaviors, clubs, committees and teams
● Overly competitive or negative team activities
● Constant complaining, griping, moaning, kvetching
● Laziness, slacking off, sleeping on the job
● Depression, anger, rage
● Plagiarism
● Falsifying reports, documents, time cards
● Developing and/or distributing potentially destructive software (viruses)
● Industrial espionage, giving away or selling company secrets and classified information
● Stealing customers
● Using company equipment/property for personal use/gain
● Unnecessary and/or unexcused absences or tardiness
● Favoritism
● Ignoring safety rules and regulations
● Name-calling and/or using sexist, racist, offensive, hurtful nick-names

NOTE: Some of these behaviors could eventually escalate to the point where they could be considered prohibited under your organization's policy and/or illegal. When in doubt, contact someone in HR/legal or a more experienced manager.

Sticky Situations. I first began working in the "soft issues" arena back in the mid 1980's while serving as part of a program development team comprised of police officers, psychologists, mental health experts, professors, professional actors and trainers. We were charged by the New York City Transit Police Department with developing and delivering a police officer training program on how to manage what cops call E.D.P.'s – emotionally disturbed persons.

One of my colleagues on the program development team, I'll call him Ted, was a very bright, articulate, creative and knowledgeable person with many, many years of professional experience in his field. Ted also happened to be an extremely intense, intimidating individual who spoke rapidly, loudly and forcefully. Ted always got in your face and looked you right in the eye when he spoke to you, and regularly insisted that you didn't know your butt from a hole in the ground. In fact, he was so intense and intimidating that it made me - and some of the others on the team - uncomfortable to be around him for very long. Ted seemed like a man on a mission and nobody was going to get in his way. Yet none of us could deny that his contributions to the program were huge and extremely valuable; Ted was truly a key player.

But Ted became even more intense as the development process moved forward and we neared the launch of the training program. It got so bad I began to dread going in to the office, even though the work we were doing was fascinating, challenging and incredibly important. I began having sleepless nights, calling in sick (which I certainly couldn't afford to do), ducking out of our meetings early, and complaining to my friends and family about how difficult it was to work with Ted. Some folks told me to get used to it, "This is the big city!" they said, while others suggested I go to Ted's boss, close the door, and talk to him about it. Everyone advised against going to Ted himself. "If he's unstable," they cautioned, "there's no telling how he'll react. He could attack you!"

Now, I think you'll agree that this was one heck of a sticky situation, and ironic. Here I was working side-by-side with someone I considered to be an emotionally disturbed person while creating a program designed to help people manage emotionally disturbed persons!

And to be honest, when I couldn't take it any longer, I did exactly what the experts on our team said I should never do: I fell apart in front of him. I completely exploded at Ted one day in the hallway outside of our offices. I yelled at him, screaming that he scared the crap out of me and that I couldn't work with him anymore. I'd had it, I was going to quit the project, and nothing could stop me. I ranted and raved like this for about two minutes, and I'm pretty sure I cried at one point. And Ted, for the first time since I'd met him, didn't say a word. He just stared at me, his mouth hanging open like a fish. After I finally finished yelling, I turned on my heel to storm away from him.

Then Ted barked out my name. I froze, with my back to him. "Why the hell didn't you say something about this three months ago?!!!!!" he shouted. "I'm not a total idiot. If you'd just told me what was bothering you, I would have stopped; saved you from making a complete fool out of yourself in front of all these people!"

Only then did I realize that our colleagues were standing in their doorways, staring at me, looking just as dumfounded as Ted. I felt like crawling into the nearest hole. "Well, I guess I should have." I stammered.

"Yup, you sure should have, you big dummy" he said. "Come back into the office and we'll work it out." And we did. In fact, we worked it out so well that after a few weeks of being hyper-careful with each other, Ted and I felt comfortable enough to tease each other. "You're not gonna start crying on me now, are you Gregg?" he'd ask, deliberately turning away from me, pretending to be sensitive to my concerns. And I'd retort with "Only if you keep acting like a total idiot."

Now even though this sticky situation ended up "okay," I sincerely hope you'll never find yourself in my shoes, having to work side-by-side with someone like Ted.   But unfortunately, it's possible you could be right now, and it's keeping you awake at night trying to figure out what to do.   "Sticky Situations" are usually those situations where you are uncomfortable, or very concerned, or at a loss as to what to do or how to respond.

Sticky situations fall into what I call the workplace "gray zone" where nothing is totally right or totally wrong, just complex, fuzzy, troubling, frustrating, difficult or emotionally loaded.   Sticky situations are sometimes the toughest things to deal with or resolve, simply because they are so damned "gray."

The best tool I can offer to help you get through sticky situations is called "The Decision Matrix" which you'll find on page 72.

Here's a partial list of sticky situations:

- Unethical business practices
- Requests for time off or overly-flexible arrangements
- Affairs
- Discovery of personal information, including medical problems
- Accidents, injuries and deaths involving employees or close relatives of employees
- Requests by employees and/or customers for preferential treatment
- Requests for transfer, salary increase, bonus or leave of absence
- Depressed or disassociative employees, colleagues and superiors
- Refusals by employees to participate in meetings, events, training or activities
- Requests from employees/customers for free goods and/or services
- Improper destruction of files/documents

- Mistakes, errors and omissions
- Stupid, inane, "knuckleheaded" comments and actions
- Deliberate obfuscation and reluctance to communicate
- Challenging, aggressive, annoying, pig-headed attitudes and comments
- Machiavellian, deceitful, undermining, sociopathic behavior
- Specific staffing requests and requests from customers for service from particular employees
- Angry, irate customers

Primer 2

What Do They Want?

*"Do unto your employees as you would have your
boss do unto you."*

Sometimes, when I think about people interacting in the workplace, I find myself humming a famous Doors tune that begins with the line, "People are strange." To me people really are strange in the sense that – more often than not – they don't behave in a logical, predictable manner. Sure, if you've practiced psychology for years, you might have a good sense of what people will do and say in a given circumstance. But for most of us lay folks, our fellow human beings are a source of bafflement, wonder and frustration.

If you're a manager, supervisor or team leader, a primary part of your job is to oversee, guide, motivate, and lead people. Sooner or later, this requires facing behaviors and situations that are totally new, strange and unexpected. I'll never forget – even though it was more than 15 years ago – how unprepared and overwhelmed I felt when one of my employees walked into my office with a black eye. Her boyfriend had beaten her up and was making threatening phone calls to her at work. I *had* to deal with that sticky situation no matter how uncomfortable it made me.

So, whether you head a group of aerospace engineers or supervise a maintenance crew, a lot of your success and satisfaction is determined by how well you work with people and can help them handle their problems. Although making assumptions about people is a dangerous practice, you should assume there are some basic things that every employee wants from their manager. What do they want from you? The same things you want from your boss.

• **Flexibility**

• **Acknowledgment**

• **Clear Expectations**

• **Trust**

It's a **F.A.C.T.** – employees want Flexibility, Acknowledgment, Clear expectations and Trust.

Flexibility. Once upon a time (most of us aren't old enough to remember it), people arrived at work around 9 am, took an hour lunch break and left around 5 pm. These were the good old days of the so-called 40-hour week. Dolly Parton even had a hit song, "Nine to Five," about it.

These days, especially in large corporations, you're hard-pressed to find anyone on salary working a mere 40 hours per week. How do I know? Since 1994, when I began doing corporate training, I've been asking managers and supervisors in each of my programs to tell me how many hours a week they typically work. Most say anywhere from 50-60 hours, and some say as many as 70. They also regularly check email and voicemail from home and while they're on vacation.

Of course, they could be inflating these numbers a bit to impress their bosses or me, but my gut tells me they're not. Additionally, many people do business while commuting, and work at all hours of the day and night from home and even on weekends (while they handle their personal responsibilities at the same time). I have a hunch, by the way, I've just described your life to you.

So, be honest, after putting in all this time, what do you want most (besides more money!) from your employer? Flexibility. Since you've given up so much of your life for work, you should get a little flexibility in return. You want to be able to come and leave when it's best for you; take a few hours off for important family events and appointments; conduct business from your home and car; and work during odd hours or weekends if you choose.

You want to be trusted with managing your time, getting your work done, and juggling all of your responsibilities like the professional you are. For some, flexibility is as important as the compensation. So, unless your employees punch a time clock, you should assume that they want the same kinds of flexibility from you as you want from your boss.

The ability to be flexible is an essential management skill, and being flexible can often produce very favorable results, increased loyalty and performance. But occasionally employees will try take advantage of you. Which brings me to the toughest part about flexibility: figuring out when to say "yes" and when to say "no."

You and I know that there's some truth to the old saying, "Give 'em an inch and they'll take a mile." Even if you've been a manager, supervisor or team leader for only a few months, you're well aware that if you're too "easy," employees may try to take advantage of you and hit you up with all sorts of frivolous requests. But if you're too strict, some employees will simply do what they want to do (without telling you!) risking disastrous results.

Last year, I got a request for flexibility that sorely tested my patience, to say the least. A member of my team was booked months in advance to travel with us by van to deliver a training program. About a week before the travel date, he called me to say that he had accepted some other work with another consulting firm which he needed to do on the same day our team was scheduled to travel. He couldn't travel with us, but he could travel on his own late in the evening and arrive in time for our presentation the next day. I was "okay" with this, and told him so. But then, he had the nerve to ask me to pay for a rental car for him and give him the per diem he would have received if he'd traveled with us in the van. I had to wonder if was he trying to take advantage, or what? I ended up giving him the per diem, but in hindsight, I think I should have said "no" to both requests. I guess I'm a bit of a sucker; I want peo-ple to like me, so I'm a little too flexible.

Here's a tool - "The Flexibility Gauge" - that might be useful to you whenever you get a request for flexibility.

The Flexibility Gauge

1. *Is It Allowed?* Is it allowed within the law and/or your organization's guide-lines?

2. *Any Increased Performance/Efficiency?* Will it result in the same performance level (or – hopefully - increased!), or efficiency, from the requesting individual?

3. *Any Negative Impact?* Will the organization itself, or other people in it, be neg-atively impacted if this request is granted?

If your answer to questions one and two is "yes," and your answer to question three is "no," you're probably on safe ground for granting the request.

However, if your answer to questions one or two is "no," or your answer to question three is "yes," then you <u>should not</u> grant the request. But, if you grant it anyway, then you must build and document a clear business case for your decision.

Whatever your reasons for granting a request for flexibility, you need to establish some "ground rules" and metrics – a way to measure the impact of the flexibility and see whether it serves your organization and goals. Insist upon a trial period for the arrangement and assess its impact regularly, if appropriate.

Best practices on flexibility

Be open to it. Let employees know you are open to reasonable requests for flexibility.

Be fair. Strike a balance between being easy and strict.

Use *The Flexibility Gauge.*

Ground rules. Establish "ground rules" and metrics - a way to measure the impact of the arrangement.

Trial period. Insist on a trial period during which you assess the arrangement regularly, if appropriate.

Acknowledgment. For three months, I worked for a woman who never acknowledged my good work, only my mistakes. She was about my age, with the same level of education and brain-power, but she had a lot less life and work experience than I did. Still, she was my boss. We'd meet on a project or proposal or budget I was working on and she'd bring a list with her of things that I'd done wrong or could potentially do wrong. She'd say, "We just need to protect the company and serve our clients." just before she skewered my mistakes. Maybe she felt she had to be tough on me to earn my respect, who knows.

But the more I worked with her, the more I lived in fear of our meetings. So, I over-compensated. I reviewed my work over and over again, making certain everything was perfect beforehand. Sure, I became very rigorous about my work, and it did improve to some extent. But she still found problems with it, and rarely, if ever, offered a word of acknowledgment. I longed for one measly, little "good job" from her, but I almost never got it. It was an awful experience. Fortunately as I said, I only worked for her for a "short time." Frustrated and unhappy, I went over her head and got myself transferred.

I've yet to meet a person who doesn't want to be acknowledged for their efforts. Everybody does – even the CEO – even you. Your people need the same; they need to be acknowledged, to hear they've performed well and met your expectations. If you fail to acknowledge people, they'll become paranoid and worried that you're not happy with them and their performance. Without acknowledgment, employees can become distracted, too eager to please, or anxious about their work.

Acknowledging the people who work for you is vital for enhancing their performance and building loyalty. A simple, "Good work," "This looks great," or "I appreciate the effort you put in." will do, even if it's about something you consider relatively unimportant. Some management experts call this a "mini-praise" or "pat on the back." But whatever it's called, consider acknowledgment to be part of your manager's toolkit.

One point to remember: *make sure your acknowledgment is sincere.* If you're being slimy or flippant while offering acknowledgment or giving too much praise too often, it will lack the "ring of truth" and backfire, causing employees to lose trust and respect for you.

Along with their good work, many employees need their emotions and feelings acknowledged. Although managers of engineers might disagree with me (just kidding), employees do have genuine emotions. Every employee is a human being with feelings and emotions that are sometimes very much in evidence. It's your job as a manager to acknowledge and be aware of your employees' emotions. While you don't have to make employees feel better if they are angry or sad or upset, you should let them know it's okay to have feelings – negative or positive. I know this sounds simplistic, but a quick "You look upset/happy," and listening to them for a minute or two is sometimes all that is needed.

All of us need our feelings acknowledged, and good managers do this in a respectful and appropriate manner. Good managers also remind us that our emotions shouldn't override our good common sense or be the sole basis of decisions.

Best practices on acknowledgment:

Regular praise. Acknowledge and praise people regularly.

Make it sincere. Offer sincere praise and acknowledgment

Acknowledge feelings: both negative and positive

Don't be run by emotions. Remind people respectfully not to be run or "ruled" by their emotions

Clear Expectations. I'll never forget working for someone who was always unclear about what he expected. He would pop into our offices to tell us frantically, "we've got a new project/assignment/initiative!" When we asked what was needed and when did it need to be done, he'd say, "You're all smart people, you figure it out." Thanks a lot, pal!

Turns out we were smart people and we usually did figure it out on our own. But we began to wonder: what the heck do we need him for and why is the company paying him more than us? So, we worked around him and he was gone in less than a year.

Most people don't perform well when expectations are unclear. In fact, in the absence of clear expectations, goals or targets, people are more likely to make mistakes, miss deadlines and generally under-perform. Employees need to know their responsibilities, what is at stake, and the schedule for completing tasks. Employees want structure, a path to follow, and realistic goals to work toward.

As a manager, it's part of your job to ensure your employees understand your expectations of them. This means regularly sitting down with employees to review their roles and responsibilities, the risks that pertain to them, the goals you want them to work toward, and the time frame in which tasks are to be completed.

Best practices on clear expectations:

Regular reviews. Regularly review and update employees' roles and responsibilities.

What's at stake? Explain what's at stake that relates to them.

Clear goals. Establish and check in on clear, specific goals.

Schedules. Establish and check in on a schedule for completion of tasks.

But please be careful; it's easy to go overboard on expectations by being too specific, and too locked into the schedule and outcomes. If you go too far, become too specific, you'll be considered the dreaded "micro-manager." People will think you don't trust them. Which leads me to...

Trust. Most people, regardless of age and experience, want to know their boss trusts them to get the job done and know what they are doing. Nobody likes a boss who hovers and micro-manages everything. In fact, most people absolutely hate it!

Whenever I lead a training seminar, I ask how many people in the class prefer to be told <u>exactly</u> what to do by their boss. On average, only 5 percent to 10 percent of respondents prefer this management style. After being given clear expectations (as described in the previous section), the vast majority of employees want to be given the benefit of the doubt that they know what they're supposed to do, can figure out on their own how to do it, and will ask for help if needed.

In my seminars on leadership, I run a short exercise I call the "Trust Discussion." I break the trainees into small groups, and then ask each person to describe to their group a business or personal relationship they have or had in which there is a very high level of trust. I ask them to talk about how that trust was developed - the specific events that helped get the relationship to that level.

People really love this exercise because they get to talk in detail about their spouse, partner, colleague, mentor, client or boss – people that mean a lot to them. But the real value in the exercise comes when the trainees realize their own high trust relationships have a lot in common with everyone else's. The light bulb goes on, and everyone realizes how important trust is to accomplishing goals and being happy in work and life.

So, how do you let your employees know that you trust them? Tell them! Make it clear from the beginning of the work relationship that you trust them to do their job and that if they do have a problem or question, they should feel free to ask you. When they do ask, invite them to suggest an answer or solution instead of simply providing it yourself.

If you encourage people to self-generate solutions or sort through problems and challenges on their own, they usually come up with viable, appropriate responses. They might even come up with a previously unknown solution that saves time and money. This, in turn, will generate more trust all around.

Best practices for generating trust:

Tell them. Let your employees know that you trust them to do their jobs.

Don't micro-manage. Avoid hovering over employees and micro-managing them.

Listen to them. Encourage employees to come to you with questions and problems

Enable them to help themselves. Encourage employees to self-generate solutions and take initiative.

But what if they make a mistake? "It's hard to trust people who make mistakes," you may be saying to yourself. If you're thinking this, remember that every employee will make a mistake, sometimes quite a few, over the course of a career. I'm sure you've made a few in your time. To err is human, nobody's perfect. However, the mistakes your employees make aren't nearly as important as your reaction to them.

A long time ago, while working as a temp for John Jay College of Criminal Justice in New York City, I mistakenly deleted a one hundred page training manual that I'd been inputting for nearly a week. I was furious at myself, but I was also terrified about how my boss, the Dean of Special Programs, would react when I told him about my mistake.

Well, he certainly cursed a blue streak; not at me, thank goodness, but at the situation in general, since we were under a strict deadline. Then he cooled down, told me to take the afternoon off to calm myself and to come back in the next day to start over. I decided on my own to come back into the office that night and I worked until dawn. We got the manual delivered on schedule. A few weeks later, the Dean offered me a permanent job in his office, which I gladly accepted. I worked with Jim Curran and John Jay College for four more terrific, interesting, challenging years.

Your employees need to know that you will not explode at them when mistakes happen. If you do explode at them – yelling and getting overly upset – they'll feel shame, think you don't trust them and will do anything to avoid your wrath in the future. And the next time they make a mistake, they'll try to hide it from you. I'm sure you agree that this is the last thing you want. As a manager, you need to know what is going on: the good, the bad and the ugly.

A more effective response to mistakes is to acknowledge that they happen from occasionally and encourage employees to self-generate solutions. If your employees know you trust them, they'll admit mistakes and often generate viable solutions on the spot. At the very least, if they know you trust them, they'll try to make it up to you somehow – like coming in to the office at night and working until dawn.

Best practices on mistakes:

Ask to be told. Ask employees to tell you about the mistakes they make.

Don't explode at them. Stay calm, avoid strong negative, blaming reactions.

You're human too. Be willing to admit your own mistakes.

Ask them to generate solutions. Encourage employees to self-generate two or three possible solutions to any mistake they make.

Be a coach, not a drill sergeant. Coach employees on finding the best solution. Allow employees the opportunity to fix their mistake.

Thank them for telling you. Always thank employees for telling you about a mistake and for finding ways to fix it.

Tell others who may be impacted. Ensure those who are directly affected by the mistake are aware of it and the solution.

Primer 3

Diversity Justified

While I was walking down a hallway in one of my clients' New York City offices on a bright Spring morning, someone waived at me through an open office door. I recognized Tom – a senior manager who had attended one of my diversity training programs a few months before. We exchanged pleasantries, and he told me how much he enjoyed my program; how much it had prompted him to think seriously about how he had been overlooking the diversity of talent within his team.

I thanked him profusely, told him he had made my day (he really had!) and turned to go. But then he quietly asked if I had a moment to talk with him about a diversity "challenge" he was having. "Sure," I said, noticing a pained expression on his face. He invited me in and closed the door firmly.

"What a view!" I couldn't help gasping as I entered Tom's office. We were on the 33rd floor, and the East River was stretched out in front of me, with a brilliant midday sun shining on the Brooklyn Bridge and the boats and water beneath it. I wanted to pause, to drink it all in for a moment. But Tom, without looking, merely grunted "thanks," and then sat down to tell me his story.

It seems that Tom was getting an enormous amount of "push-back" from Richard, a very successful, long-time, top-selling, leader in the organization. Richard was refusing to serve on a new team assigned to develop an interactive e-commerce web site. From what Tom could sense during their short, painful discussions, Richard was embarrassed by his lack of technical knowledge and skills – for example, he was a hunt-and-peck typist and had trouble booting up his own computer.

Of course Richard wouldn't actually admit his embarrassment, he just danced around it, making excuses about why he wouldn't be available to serve on the team. And, trying to convince Tom that he wouldn't "fit in," Richard referred to the entire e-commerce site development team as "that bunch of young turks."

But Tom and everyone else at the company was well aware that Richard was one hell of a salesman. He was the company's best, earning well over a million dollars a year in salary and commissions. He had experience, knowledge and contacts that would be incredibly valuable to that development team.

So even though Richard had ample experience with the sales process and the clients, he was flat out refusing to help in the one place where all that knowledge would be incredibly useful. And to make matters worse, after Tom pushed back on Richard's push-back, Richard began amplifying his excuses: "I don't have the time," he would say, "I'm always on the road and unavailable," and "my seniority exempts me from 'techie' assignments."

Visibly frustrated after telling me about Richard's excuses, Tom leaned toward me, "Without Richard, that group could make some serious and really expensive mistakes." I noticed I could count at least four deep worry lines across Tom's forehead. "Gregg, we may never recover from those mistakes. What the hell do I do?!"

Right there, it became clear to me that Tom was caught in what I call the "diversity gray zone," where a people problem is a complex psychological, socio-logical and political puzzle. Once you're inside the diversity gray zone, it's really hard to figure out how to get out. You can get yourself all tangled up into knots in there, and deep worry lines can embed themselves in your forehead.

What is "diversity"? Not very long ago, when asked to define "diversity," most people said the word referred to race and gender differences, glass ceilings, and/or affirmative action and quotas. Some folks still see it this way, and I suspect they always will because they're stuck in a discriminatory environment, or closed-minded, or locked into a particular political/ideological position on diversity.

Fortunately, in many workplaces, the definition of diversity has broadened considerably. We've reached the point where a majority of employees are aware that the term – while certainly including race and gender – goes way beyond them to include many, many different things: *age, birth order, disability, education, ethnicity, generation, life/work experiences, marital status, national origin, parental status, personality, physical attributes, political views, religion, sexual orientation, skills, socioeconomic status, and veteran status,* to name just a few. I could go on forever adding to this list of differences.

It's obvious that every workplace is filled with diversity – different types of people with different backgrounds, skills, experiences, education, personalities, attitudes, work habits, behaviors and ideas. What's not so obvious is that your success and the success of your organization depend almost entirely on how you and your fellow managers <u>value and leverage</u> this diversity. If you and your colleagues do it well, you will see many tangible and intangible benefits. If you don't, the costs could be heavy.

The Diversity Target/Wheel. While leading diversity training seminars, I often use a simple graphic (some trainers call it "the diversity target" or "diversity wheel chart") to explain the concept of individual differences.

Imagine that this bulls-eye target below represents you. When someone meets you for the first time, they immediately learn things about you based upon the attributes found in the outermost ring – your so-called "Visible" or "Surface" diversity - gender, race, age, physical attributes and so on.

After a period of time, people eventually get to know more about you by learning about your "Invisible" diversity," – your skills, experiences, religion, education, etc. – all found in the second ring on the target. Finally, they get to know you by learning about what I call your "Core Diversity" – your character or personality, your work style and personal "truths" about life, work and the world. You'll see those in the innermost ring – the hub - of the wheel.

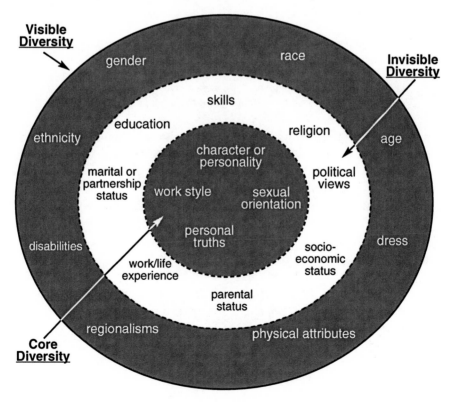

The core diversity issues are extremely important to be aware of because they have a huge impact on how we interact with others. They are often the primary determinants on how an interaction with another person or group is likely to play out.

But please don't misunderstand; I'm not minimizing the role that "Visible Diversity" factors play in daily interactions. I am well aware that when a black man, or a woman, or a very overweight person walks into a room, regardless of how well people know them, everyone in the room still sees a black man, or a woman, or a very overweight person walking into the room. Sadly, in many instances, people interact with others solely within the context of the visible or surface diversity.

Nevertheless the core diversity factors – work style, personal truths, personality - are so significant that countless individuals, psychologists, sociologists, colleges, universities and laboratories have committed more than 100 years of academic research, study and measurement to understanding them.

But forget about academia. Overall, when it comes to work, the two most important things every manager, supervisor or team leader needs to "get" about diversity are:

• Diversity should be valued and leveraged so that individuals and their organizations can meet their goals and succeed; and

• Diversity will be successfully valued and leveraged only in those organizations that have an <u>inclusive</u> management culture.

Leveraging Diversity. What does the term "leveraging diversity" mean and why is it so important? First, we need to know which diversity we're talking about, as the term refers to organizations: "Internal Diversity" or "External Diversity."

Internal diversity refers to the diversity " inside your organization," all the employees, vendors and partners – the people who need to work together in order to get the job done. External diversity refers to the diversity "outside of your organization," your customers and clients – the people your organization serves.

If you're leveraging internal diversity, you're making use of all the skills, experiences, relationships and other unique attributes of your employees, vendors and partners.

If you're leveraging external diversity, you're targeting specific groups and markets, customizing your products and services to serve them specifically and, as a result, increasing your overall market share and revenues.

In today's new, new economy, most organizations "get" the business case for leveraging external diversity. The numbers and demo-graphics tell us why they get it so readily. In 2013, California announced that the number of Latinos will match the number of non-Hispanic whites for the first time. The Latino consumer market in the U.S. is growing extremely rapidly and there are more African Americans in the middle and upper middle classes than ever before. Emerging markets including China and the former Soviet Union are potential gold mines for companies selling consumer goods and services. Is it any wonder many major U.S. companies lobbied feverishly to give China Most-Favored-Nation trading status? Most business leaders know that companies, especially retailers, that don't aggressively target diverse customer groups are going to see declines in market share and revenues. So, given the numbers and changing demographics, it's easy for most organizations to establish a benchmark on external diversity and then measure their success at leveraging it. That's why they "get it" on external diversity.

However, what's harder for many business leaders to get, let alone explain, is the business case rationale for leveraging internal diversity. This is because there are so many intangible and subjective factors at play within it: productivity, customer and employee satisfaction, turnover, complaints, compensation, return-on-investment for training, you name it. Bottom line, it's much harder to benchmark and measure the impact of leveraging internal diversity. It can be done, and some companies are doing it, but I'll be the first to admit that developing met-rics around internal diversity takes a lot of effort, and the results can be fuzzy.

I can only imagine how overwhelming this must seem to the average manager. "How the heck can I get with the program on leveraging inter-nal diversity," you may be thinking, "if progress is so hard to measure and benefits are so intangible?" Well, the easiest way for individual managers to leverage internal diversity is to start small, by working with individual team members.

Margie. For example, we've already established that your team is comprised of unique individuals with unique skills, experiences, knowl-edge and expertise. Imagine you have someone on your team, Margie, who processes and ships orders for your company – "order fulfillment."

To do this, Margie uses a specific software application on her computer. But much to your consternation, she and many of the others in your company regularly complain that the software they are using is, in a word, "junk."

Then one day during casual conversation you find out that Margie had taken a computer course on how to write code for software applications. Smart manager that you are, you ask Margie to take a look at the current software to see if she can improve it, or at least do a cost/benefit analysis to determine if it should be replaced with something better. You let Margie know that doing so will be helpful to her personally and possibly to everyone else. Margie may respond by asking for additional compensation or a bonus for doing this work, and you'll probably have to negotiate that with her.

But in the end, Margie does have some success with the software, and you have leveraged her diversity so that it helps the organization. The measurable results? You reduced the time it takes Margie and her colleagues to fulfill orders, and this in turn increased overall productivity and morale. As I said, some success you can measure, some you can't.

Getting back to my friend Tom's problem, as you can imagine, valuing Richard's diversity was easy: the man had a lot of useful knowledge and experience, Tom knew about it and wanted it to be put to work on the e-commerce team. But actually leveraging Richard's diversity was another matter entirely since he was adamantly refusing to play nicely in the sandbox with the "young Turks."

In this situation, it's pretty easy for Tom to measure the results if he leverages Richard's diversity and to guess what's going to happen if he doesn't. Success means the e-commerce team has access to an incredibly valuable resource at their fingertips, which they could leverage to create one heck of a web presence Without Richard, the team and the company could waste and lose some serious money, not to mention blow the opportunity to generate new revenues.

I call the following on-paper exercise a "Diversity Cost/Benefit Analysis." It's a simple tool for identifying the benefits of succeeding in a particular course of action. It also helps you identify the costs of failure in that particular course of action.

Imagine you're my friend Tom, trying to determine the benefits of getting Richard to work with the e-commerce team, and the cost of him not working with the team. Start by asking yourself the question, "What happens if...? "

What happens if...

"I leverage Richard's diversity"	"I don't leverage his diversity."
Benefits:	*Costs:*
- The e-commerce team has experienced help	- They're up a creek w/out paddle
- New customers have their needs met	- Hit or miss with new customers
- Costly development mistakes avoided	- Here's hoping they won't blow it
- New source of revenue opens up	- No idea if revenues will come
- I look good to top brass	- I look like poop to top brass

After doing this Diversity Cost/Benefit Analysis you can probably understand why Tom had such deep worry lines in his forehead.

The End State Statement. To help Tom pry himself loose from the diversity gray zone, I asked him to come up with what I call an "End State Statement," or E.S.S. (see page 77) The E.S.S. is a one-sentence snapshot of the specific future you want to see.

Tom said, "My E.S.S. is: *Richard is an enthusiastic and on-call resource to the e-commerce development team.*"

Then, Tom and I brainstormed a bunch of strategies that Tom might use to have his E.S.S. become a reality. Here's what our brainstorming session came up with:

1. Get Richard to see that working on the new e-commerce project team will benefit him personally – financially? New title? Bonus? Award?

2. Offer Richard technical training and send him to "E-commerce 101".

3. Threaten Richard with the loss of his job.

4. Beg Richard to help, ask him to do a personal favor.

5. Make him a financial offer he can't refuse.

6. Give up and pray the team can do it without Richard's help.

Finally, I asked Tom to use "The Decision Matrix" (see page 72) to help him make a decision as to what to do. After using the matrix, Tom decided he was going to try a combination of the first and second strategies: put a bunch of personal incentives in front of Richard and pay for training to get him up to speed. I also advised Tom to be very specific with Richard as to what was expected of him. About a year later, Tom let me know he succeeded in leveraging Richard's diversity and the team built a "hot" e-commerce web site with his help. It's generating revenue, he added. Not as much as they'd projected, but it's definitely in the black.

Mike. About two years ago, I developed a diversity training program for an insurance company that was run almost exclusively by a group of middle aged, heterosexual white males. My team and I flew in from New York to present the program at their annual sales manager's conference. Except for a couple of women and minorities, the room was filled with nearly a hundred middle-aged white guys in dark suits. Our job was to convince this group about the personal and business benefits of valuing and leveraging diversity; to convince them of the so-called "business case."

To be honest, when we walked into the room and eyeballed the audience, we thought we really had our work cut out for us. And as we suspected, they were a chilly bunch. The problem wasn't with our program, which they seemed to enjoy and find interesting, but with the fact that we were outsiders delivering a hard-to-swallow message to an exclusive club of insiders.

Then at the end of our program, as we were about to take our leave, an Executive VP of Sales with the company – a white guy in his 50's named Mike – came down to the front to speak, to wrap things up. I'd met Mike once before, and learned that he was one of the top earners for the firm, a "Best Salesman Award" winner, year after year. He was a big, burly, gregarious man who really filled out his suit. I figured he was probably worth $10 to $20 million, at least.

But now Mike seemed very nervous as he walked to the podium, and his voice cracked as he began to speak. Surprising us all, he announced that our program had moved him very deeply and as a result, there was something he felt he needed to tell them. He said it was something that he'd never spoken of in public before. I thought, "My god, he's coming out of the closet!" Wrong. Instead, Mike said something that confounded me for a moment. Heck, it confounded us all.

"I really want to praise our company for how it uses diversity," he said. "Because if our company didn't value and leverage diversity, then I wouldn't be where I am today." Well, how the heck could that be, we all wondered. Mike is one of the straight-white-male ruling elite in this company. Of all people, he surely didn't need his diversity valued and leveraged.

Then Mike stunned us. While his voice quavered with emotion, he admitted that throughout his childhood he had been "dirt poor." He told us he'd been raised in a trailer park in central Kentucky and that every day at school the other kids teased him, calling him "trailer trash," "redneck," "white trash," and "hillbilly." By this point, Mike's eyes had welled up with tears, and everyone in the room was sitting motionless, riveted.

Mike said that the moment he graduated high school he left Kentucky forever and moved to Los Angeles with just a few dollars in his pocket. He was hired by this company to sell term life insurance on commission only out of a storefront in one of the poorest neighborhoods in LA. Within a few months, the company made him a manager over a team comprised of young, inexperienced salesmen - almost all of whom were African-American, Asian or Hispanic – all desperately trying to make it in a dog-eat-dog business.

The day he was made a manager, Mike explained, he adopted one simple rule for his team. And it was this rule, he was convinced, that enabled his team to transform itself into one of the most successful sales groups in the history of the company. That rule? "One for all and all for one."

Mike then reminded us that this occurred nearly 30 years ago, long before "diversity" became a trendy buzzword in corporations. And then he stunned us all once more by issuing this warning, and his whole body shook as he spoke: "Don't you ever let your team down. Don't you ever forget to value every bit of them. Always be there for them, always support them. I don't care if they are black, white, gay, straight, old, young, disabled or poor, snot-nosed kids from a trailer park in Kentucky. You give them everything you've got. You work for them, and they will work for you." Then Mike's voice became suddenly quiet and small, and he excused himself for becoming too emotional. He politely thanked them for listening and started to walk away from the podium.

Well, as you can imagine, the room completely erupted. Everyone jumped up from their seats, some crying, some cheering, all applauding Mike like he was the President of the United States. Then it was Mike's turn to be stunned as people rushed down the aisles to clap him on the back, shake his hand, and congratulate him personally. It was a real honest-to-goodness "love in." And, given that this group was the crème de la crème of a stuffy Yankee insurance company, I wouldn't have believed it if I hadn't seen it with my own eyes.

That is clearly a good story about a manager who values and leverages diversity. But I'm sorry to say, in some organizations the very idea of diversity, not to mention valuing and leveraging it, has been maligned, dismissed, misrepresented, misunderstood and undermined for lots of different reasons, many of which are just plain rotten, including racism, sexism, ageism, all the "isms."

Add to this: diversity training programs that beat up on white males; the media's narrow-minded focus on what I call "diversity conflicts," (class action law suits, affirmative action legislation, glass ceiling complaints); the us-versus-them mentality between labor and management; exclusive, elitist management cultures that talk-the-talk on diversity but don't really walk it, and you've got a whole lot of trouble in a lot of companies where people don't feel valued or listened to at all.

In many organizations you'll find a number of senior managers who are busy burying their heads in the sand on diversity, or hiding their resistance to change behind their balance sheets, or playing political games and jockeying for position and power. Theirs is an exclusive culture. They don't really get it on diversity, and they don't want to get it because valuing and leveraging diversity asks them to fundamentally change they way they operate - to be inclusive rather than exclusive.

In fact, although they'll never admit it, some top managers see diversity as a threat to their authority, their fiefdoms and their very way of life. So clever folks that they are, they talk-the-talk on diversity, but they don't dare walk it. I've even seen one top manager give a rousing and impassioned town meeting speech about valuing diversity, and then the very next day, while considering a short list of candidates for a senior position, I overheard him exclaim, "We don't need to look at the 'diversity candidates' for this slot, none of them will be any good."

This kind of attitude is even more damaging than not talking about diversity at all. In some companies, the hypocrisy on diversity has gotten so bad that the very word itself has become politically charged. It's become like foul language - the dreaded "d-word."

Some of my clients, who really value the diversity training my group provides them, insist that we don't publicize our program as diversity training. "Call it anything else," they say, "but don't call it 'diversity training' until you actually have them in the training room." So when we promote our diversity training at these organizations, we call it "team-building," "maximizing teams," "organizational development," "synergistic leveraging," and so on.

Whatever it's called, valuing and leveraging diversity are extremely important skills for any manager. Let me put it another way; in this new millennium, managers that don't leverage diversity are running a serious risk.

If you fail to value and leverage the diversity of your team, here's what's likely to happen:

- You will fail to meet your goals entirely, or you'll meet them with difficulty and behind schedule.
- You'll miss or overlook opportunities to increase revenues.
- You'll see poor productivity, performance and retention rates.
- You'll experience higher turnover and complaints.
- Generally you will feel overwhelmed, unsupported and unhappy.

Consider the retention issue. Everyone says they want to retain the best employees, but that it's often very hard to do. Agreed, it is hard. But failing to retain the best is going to cost a great deal. According to the international outplacement firm of Lee Hecht Harrison, the average cost of replacing an employee - when factoring direct costs such as severance packages and indirect costs such as recruitment, time lost by their team and retraining - is two and a half times the employee's annual salary. That's no small chunk of change. Of course, employees leave for all sorts of reasons – some personal, some professional. And some of these reasons may have nothing to do with whether or not their manager leveraged their diversity.

But, as a manager, the last thing you want to hear is that your employees are leaving because they didn't feel valued, listened to or rewarded for their contributions. If they're saying things like this in exit interviews, then they really mean they think your company is a lousy place to work. Bottom line: you will retain valuable employees by leveraging their diversity. This saves money, increases morale, productivity and revenues.

Another interesting statistic related to internal diversity: 69 percent of committed employees reported that respectful treatment is the factor most likely to convince them to continue working for their current employers (see chapter notes). Likewise, in a study of executives from the nation's 1000 largest companies, corporate culture was cited as the main motive for staying with an organization (see chapter notes).

We could go on forever looking at the data supporting the concepts of valuing and leveraging diversity. But instead, I want to make one last point about this by quoting Bill Stasior, former CEO of the consulting group Booz Allen Hamilton. He summed it up perfectly during an off-site meeting I was facilitating recently. "Valuing and leveraging diversity," he said, "is simply the right thing to do."

Here is a typical diversity cost/benfit analysis that applies to most managers:

Manager's Cost/Benefit Analysis: VALUING & LEVERAGING DIVERSITY

If you fail to leverage the diversity of your team, you will...

• Continue to have difficulty recruiting and retaining the best people.

• Operate as a lone ranger, risking personal overwhelm, inefficiency and frustration.

• Miss opportunities to grow the business in ways you never thought possible.

• Put your "numbers" at risk in ways you never thought possible.

• Have a team that is under-motivated and under-utilized.

• Put yourself at risk, jeopardizing advancement and promotion.

If you work at leveraging the diversity of your team, you will...

• Find it easier to recruit and retain the best people.

• Cease operating as a "lone ranger", lowering your sense of overwhelm, inefficiency and frustration.

• Discover opportunities to grow the business in new ways.

• Lower the risk of not meeting your "numbers."

• Be supported by a team which is motivated.

That Personality Thing. As you can see from the diversity target, your personality is at the core of your diversity. Most of us have a pretty good sense of our personality and how others perceive us. And most of us try to cooperate with our co-workers and treat them with respect. Unfortunately every work group has at least one member with a "strong" personality; somebody who thinks they are the center of the universe, who talks too much, is a know-it-all, or bossy, or rude, or manipulative, or just downright mean and nasty. This kind of behavior can be a real pain and a drain on everyone's time and energy. And it's unbelievable how many people with strong personalities haven't a clue as to how much their behavior is negatively impacting the group.

Last year I facilitated some senior executive meetings in which I came face-to-face with someone with a very strong personality. This individual, I'll call him Dick, was driving us all to distraction with his rude and disrespectful behavior. During presentations and briefings he would engage in sidebar conversations, interrupt presenters constantly to ask questions or give his ego-inflated opinion, and generally act like he was the most important person on the planet. During one session, when the presenter asked him to stop his sidebar conversation and pay attention, Dick became irate and stormed from the room. We all breathed a sigh a relief and went on with the meeting, which went much more smoothly from there.

So, what are we to do about people like Dick? Well, we shouldn't ignore their bad behavior and say "that's just the way they are." Pyschologists would call us "enablers" if we did. I'd say we're just wimps. Plain truth; negative behavior by people with strong personalities is too destructive, demoralizing and demotivating to be ignored. But on the other hand, it almost never rises to a level that begs for formal disciplinary action.

Instead, most people think that "someone should take Dick aside and talk to him." That's exactly right. Someone does need to talk to him, but it has to be the right someone. People with strong personalities find it hard to be "talked to" or coached about their behavior. They don't want to hear it, because they've heard it all before from their friends, spouses, old colleagues and bosses. It didn't sink in then, and it's not going to sink in now. So if someone you work with needs coaching on their strong personality traits, you must find a colleague s/he trusts. Usually, this is a colleague who has worked with the person for a long time. Or it could be the person's current boss if – and this is imperative – there's a high level of trust between them.

Once the talker/coach has been identified, s/he should choose an appropriate time and location for the coaching session. Yelling at the offender in public while s/he's doing her/his thing is definitely not going to help change the behavior. In fact, this will probably make it worse. An appropriate time and place for coaching might be after work or during a break, at a restaurant or park - someplace "neutral" where the offender won't feel threatened.

The talk itself should follow along the lines of the "Coaching Your Colleague" tool on page 75 and should include the "Changed Man Technique" on page 70. No one other than the offender

and the coach should be present at this session. In fact, only a few people should even know it is going to occur. If the offender finds out
her/his colleagues are excitedly looking forward to the big day s/he gets
coached, then the whole process will be completely undermined and the
behavior could easily go from bad to worse.

Once the coaching session is done, it would be best if no one made
any reference to it at all. An occassional compliment in the person's
direction wouldn't hurt, but everyone needs to guard against going overboard. Saying, "You sure have turned into a nice person since so-and-so
chewed you out," is probably not going to help.

Sure, people with personalities like Dick's can drive us all insane,
and it's hard not to become passionately righteous about how awful they
are to work with. But physician, heal thyself. Before you start complaining about the strong personality in your work group, take a good
look in the mirror and make sure it's not you.

Primer 4

Harassment in a Nutshell

See it or hear it?
Report it and document it!

Is It or Isn't It? Last year I got a call from Dan – the head of a pharmaceutical sales group – who asked me to advise him on a little problem he was having with two of his sales managers, a man and a woman. They were colleagues, long-time employees, top earners, and extremely well liked and respected. The problem? Although he couldn't prove it, Dan's "gut" told him that they were having an affair.

Dear reader: does this alleged affair constitute workplace harassment, or hostile work environment, or not?

Tough question. Pose this situation and question to a thousand different employment law attorneys and you'll probably get a thousand different answers. Remember, I'm no attorney, I just work with them. My layman's answer: I don't think so, but it could be considered hostile work environment if one of them directly supervises the other, or their behavior negatively impacts others in the company.

But Dan made it clear to me that they were colleagues of the same rank and that there wasn't even a whisper of gossip about these two having an affair. It was only his gut that was telling him something was going on, nothing else.

My initial response threw Dan for a loop. "I think you should keep your nose out of it," I said bluntly. "It's none of your business if they are having an affair."

"But they're married," he blurted out, "And not to each other! And they both have kids, and, and...well, it's just plain immoral!" Unfortunately for him, Dan was preaching to the wrong choir. I'm not very tolerant of managers who judge their employees' private and personal behavior by their own moral code. So I told Dan to put a cork in his dudgeon and spend his time worrying about the people in his group who were screwing up their work.

"That's totally the opposite of what our legal department told me to do," Dan retorted. "They want to jump on it immediately, to protect the company from possible litigation."

Now I was the one thrown for a loop. "If you've already been advised by your lawyers," I asked, "what the heck are you calling me for?"

There was a long pause, then he said quietly, "A second opinion." adding that he was now more confused than ever about what to do. Talk about bad behavior, people problems and a sticky situation all rolled into one!

Apparently, the company's attorneys wanted to draw up some kind of legal document for the couple to sign, a "love contract," they called it. This document would make it clear to the couple that if they were engaging in adulterous acts on company or client property, or arranging to do so on company time or equipment (computers, phones, etc.) and these acts or actions were proven by the company to have occurred, then they would be grounds for disciplinary action, up to and including termination. The document was also intended to indemnify the company from anything that might occur if the relationship ever became public, or soured, or if one of them became a supervisor to the other.

On hearing this, I did what every smart consultant should do, I chickened out and deferred to the lawyers.

But I challenged Dan to consider how asking the love birds to sign such a contract would impact his business. "Well, it's certainly going to be embarrassing for them." he said, "And it will probably hurt their secret relationship – which might not be such a bad thing for them or their families." "Dan," I cautioned sharply, "you're moralizing again. Stick to the business consequences of this particular course of action."

Dan cursed, admitting that this was "one hell of a sticky situation!" (I didn't challenge him on the cursing – you've got to know when to pick your fights.) As he thought out loud about it, Dan became certain that being asked to sign such a document would "really freak them out." They could resign because of it, he mused, and that would really hurt business. If they signed the contract and stayed with the firm, then their sense of humiliation and shame and overall emotion-al state might impact their ability to do their jobs as well as they had been doing, at least for a while. "That could really hurt the team, and our clients, and our revenues." Now he was thinking like the good man-ager that I knew him to be.

In the end Dan decided to reject his lawyer's advice *and* my advice. As we talked, he came up with a third option, which was to privately approach one of the two, the one he knew best, and talk with them off-the-record and confidentially, "as a friend." He was going to ask him or her to consider all of the implications an extra-marital affair might have on their lives, their careers, their colleagues, and their families. He intended to recommend privately that they end the affair. Dan seemed satisfied that this was the best way to handle it and asked me what I thought. I replied that it was a very well crafted "Clintonian" third way, and wished him luck with it.

I saw Dan a few months later and asked him what had happened. He said he'd spoken to one of them and it was the most difficult discussion he'd ever had with an employee. But as far as he could tell, the relationship ended shortly thereafter. As for the lawyers, Dan told them he was mistaken, and to shred the contract. "But," he added with a wink, "just to protect myself, I documented the whole thing in a secure file that only I know about."

Where are we now? Has today's work environment changed much since the 1960's and 70's when chasing a secretary around the desk, giving sexually provocative gifts, and taking clients to a strip club were pretty much the norm? Maybe it has, since most companies these days wouldn't tolerate behavior like that for a nano-second. But, on the other hand, almost every day, headlines tell about yet another company paying hundreds of thousands, if not millions, of dollars worth of settlements, damages and legal expenses resulting from the inappropriate and offensive behavior of its employees and managers. So, have things really changed, or not?

Yes and no. The reality is even though the egregious and overt harassing behavior has been reduced significantly in most work environments, there's still plenty of inappropriate, offensive and illegal stuff going on.

Every day, millions of people e-mail sexually and racially offensive jokes, pornographic photos, and cartoons to each other at work or use the foulest of foul language during meetings and conference calls. In many work environments nasty, abusive remarks about so-and-so's body, clothing and makeup or comments like, "what a slut she is," are commonplace. Thousands of people (mostly women) are offered raises, promotions and bonuses in exchange for sexual favors. Some folks deliberately choose not to wear underwear beneath short skirts and tight pants while at work (I kid you not!). Others spend break-time spinning elaborate stories about their sexual exploits. Gropes, pinches, gestures, insults, foul and sexually charged language, catcalls, and wolf whistles remain everyday occurrences in many workplaces.

I'm only talking about the U.S. here. I lived in Europe for many years during the 1980's and 90's and I'm very sorry to report that the rest of the world is no better, and oftentimes worse, than the U.S in identifying and addressing inappropriate and offensive behavior.

Anyone can harass anyone else. Sexual harassment is not just about men harassing women; it can be about women harassing men, men harassing men and women harassing women. Now, of course, men will always complain that sexual harassment training programs usually focus on men harassing women, but that's because of many factors related to the history of the workplace and relations between the two genders since time began. Reality check: most sexual harassment complaints are made by women against men, and in most cases, men are the offenders. Sadly, due to subconscious cultural programming, most men find it extremely difficult to file a complaint of harassment against another man, or a woman for that matter.

In my harassment prevention training programs I quote EEOC (Equal Employment Opportunity Commission) statistics from the mid 1990's that indicate roughly three (3) percent of all employees have been the direct targets of harassment or gender-based discrimination. Most of my trainees scoff at that percentage, thinking it's much higher. Some human resources folks I know say they believe 20 to 30 percent is a more accurate figure.

In my programs I certainly don't ask for a show of hands of those who have been targeted. But judging by the look on people's faces and the nodding of heads after I tell them what my human resources friends think, I believe it's safe to assume the real number is much higher than three (3) percent. Most experts agree that that vast majority of incidents are unreported.

The List. Every time I lead a program on workplace harassment, the trainees ask me for "The List." They want the comprehensive list of permitted and prohibited language and behaviors. People want to know exactly what they can and cannot do. And they especially want the people sitting next to them in the training room – people who are perceived to be harassers – to see "the list."

I sincerely wish I could provide such a list to them. But, unfortunately, it doesn't exist, for many reasons.

First, even though every state in the union has laws on harassment, many states' harassment laws are unique to themselves. Some states, for example, prohibit discrimination and harassment based on sexual orientation, while others do not. On top of this, in almost every state in the union, if you look back over the last couple of decades, you'll find that the concepts of harassment and discrimination are constantly shifting targets. In other words everything is in flux.

Laws are being changed, reinterpreted, discarded, appealed, and updated almost continuously. Even within a given state, jurisdiction or courtroom, harassment laws are interpreted differently by different human resources experts, companies, lawyers, prosecutors, judges, and juries. Some judges take verbal harassment very seriously, while others think it's a waste of court time. Since federal laws are generally less strict than state laws, they don't really help either. From where I see it, trying to make a comprehensive, understandable list of do's and don'ts out of this legal quagmire is an invitation to a Sisyphean nightmare.

Secondly, if you do manage to cobble together some kind of comprehensive list, you'll find it immediately falling prey to the human desire to bend the rules, get around boundaries and prohibitions, and push the proverbial envelope.

There's an infamous story from the 1980s that illustrates this perfectly. A reputable consulting group was contracted to provide harassment and diversity training to all the employees of a large public utility. Before rolling out the training, the consultants conducted a survey to determine what employees considered appropriate and inappropriate language and behavior. This survey resulted in a massive list that was handed over to the utility's legal counsel for review and comment. After the lawyers justified their fees by contributing a few choice ideas of their own, the completed list was handed out to the first group of trainees on the first day of training.

Reportedly, the trainees sat and studied this list in silence for about 10 minutes, while the consultants patted themselves on the back for covering all the bases. But then, one by one, hands started to go up in the training room. People had questions.

"I don't see the word **** on the prohibited language list," someone asked using some choice local slang, "So I guess that's okay, right?" Then someone else demonstrated a particular hand gesture that they couldn't find on the list. Others jumped in enthusiastically with more questions, contributions and ideas – transforming the class into a veritable smorgasbord of offensive language and behaviors. Within a few minutes the comprehensive list that the consultants worked so diligently to assemble had become completely obsolete. The moral of the story: *the list of do's and don'ts you put together today will be out of date tomorrow.*

Nevertheless, if you feel you have to see a list - any list- your safest bet is to look at your organization's harassment policy. It should include some kind of descriptive language that covers inappropriate, prohibited and/or illegal behavior.

The following is what I consider to be a well-written and solid anti-harassment policy. I've placed it here in the book, rather than at the back, because I'd like you to read it now.

XYZ Company's Anti-Harassment Policy. XYZ Company intends to provide a work environment that is pleasant, professional, and free from intimidation, hostility or other offenses that might interfere with work performance. Harassment against employees of any sort - verbal, physical and visual - will not be tolerated, particularly on the basis of race, color, religion, sex, age, sexual orientation, national origin or ancestry, disability, medical condition, marital status, parental status, veteran status, or any other characteristic.

What Is Harassment?   Harassment is unwelcome verbal, visual or physical conduct that creates an intimidating, offensive or hostile work environment which interferes with work performance. Examples of harassment include verbal (including slurs, jokes, insults, epithets, gestures, or teasing), graphic (including offensive posters, symbols, cartoons, drawings, computer displays or e-mails) or physical conduct (including physically threatening another, blocking someone's way, etc.) that denigrates or shows hostility or aversion toward an individual because of any protected characteristic. Such conduct constitutes harassment when: (1) it has the purpose or effect of creating an intimidating, hostile, or offensive work environment; or (2) it has the purpose or effect of unreasonably interfering with an individual's work performance; or (3) it otherwise adversely affects an individual's employment opportunities.

Responsibility and Reporting. All XYZ Company employees, and particularly managers, have a responsibility for keeping our work environment free of harassment. Any employee who becomes aware of an incident of harassment by witnessing or being told of it, must report it to their immediate manager or any other manager with whom they feel comfortable. If an employee is unsure about who they should go to raise an issue about harassment, Human Resources at (800) ***-**** should be contacted immediately. HR will insure the incident is immediately investigated. Managers are required to report any incident of harassment to the HR Department or be subject to discipline up to and including termination. When management becomes aware of the existence of harassment, it is obligated to take prompt and appropriate action, whether or not the target of the harassment wants the company to do so.

All reports of perceived harassment will be fully investigated with due regard for the privacy of everyone involved. However, confidentiality cannot be guaranteed. Any employee found to have harassed a fellow employee, subordinate, vendor, or customer will be subject to disciplinary action up to and including termination. XYZ Company will also take any additional action necessary to appropriately remedy the situation. Retaliation of any sort will not be permitted. No adverse employment action will be taken against any employee, witnesses, or confidants who make a good faith report of alleged harassment.

Failure to report incidents of harassment makes it impossible for XYZ Company to cure the problem or prevent future instances of harassment.

Policy Statement on Sexual Harassment. What Is Sexual Harassment? Sexual harassment may include unwelcome sexual advances, requests for sexual favors, or other verbal or physical contact of a sexual nature when such conduct creates an offensive, hostile and intimidating working environment or prevents an individual from effectively performing the duties of his or her position. It also encompasses such conduct when it is made a term or condition of employment or compensation, either implicitly or explicitly and when an employment decision is based on an individual's acceptance or rejection of such conduct. It is important to note that sexual harassment crosses age and gender boundaries and cannot be stereotyped.

Sexual harassment may exist on a continuum of behavior. For instance, one example of sexual harassment may be that of an employee showing offensive pictures to another employee.

Generally, two categories of sexual harassment exist. The first - "quid pro quo" - may be defined as an exchange of sexual favors for improvement in working conditions and/or compensation. The second - "hostile, intimidating, offensive working environment" - can be described as a situation in which unwelcome sexual advances, or requests for sexual favors are made, or other verbal or physical contact of a sexual nature when such conduct creates an intimidating or offensive environment. Examples of a hostile, intimidating, and offensive working environment include:

• Unwelcome sexual advances, flirtations, leering, whistling, touching, pinching, assault, or blocking normal movement;
• Requests for sexual favors or demands for sexual favors in exchange for favorable treatment;
• Obscene or vulgar gestures, posters or comments;

- Sexual jokes, or comments about a person's body, sexual prowess or sexual deficiencies;
- Propositions, or suggestive or insulting comments of a sexual nature;
- Visual harassment such as derogatory cartoons, posters and drawings;
- Sexually explicit e-mail or voice mail;
- Touching of a sexual nature;
- "Sexually loaded" comments;
- Conversation about one's own or someone else's sex life;
- Conduct or comments consistently targeted at only one gender, even if the content is not sexual;
- Teasing or other conduct directed toward a person because of his or her gender;
- Downloading or transmittal of non-work related, inappropriate or offensive pictures or materials on computer systems.

Harassing conduct is unacceptable in the workplace and any work-related setting such as business trips and business related functions. The harasser may be someone's supervisor, co-worker, subordinate, client, customer, vendor, or other third party.

Retaliation. XYZ Company prohibits any employee from retaliating in any way against anyone who has raised any concern about sexual harassment or discrimination against another individual.

Investigation. Every report of harassment will be investigated thoroughly and promptly. XYZ Company will attempt to keep the investigation confidential to the extent possible. During the investigation, XYZ Company will generally:

- Interview the complainant and alleged harasser;
- Conduct further interviews as necessary;
- Document the Company's finding regarding the complaint;
- Document recommended follow-up actions and remedies if warranted;
- Inform the complainant of the Company's findings and where appropriate, of the remedial action that will be taken.

The Manager's Responsibilities. Notice that this policy makes it very clear that incidents you witness or are told about must be reported immediately. This is particularly important for managers and supervisors to understand, because today more than ever, employers hold managers and supervisors responsible for the actions of employees. You are expected to know what's going on with the people who report to you. If you fail to report incidents, it's likely that your organization will hold you responsible. And in some states, it is possible – not probable but still possible – you could be sued in civil court if plaintiff's attorneys perceive there is money to be made from you.

You see a lot of the hoopla around harassment is about money. As I said in my introduction, we in the United States live in the most litigious society in the history of civilization. More people are suing each other and their employers than ever before, and there seems to be no end in sight. When it comes to lawsuits, "Who has got the deep pockets?" is what plaintiffs' attorneys always want to know.

Now I'm not saying harassment doesn't occur. Of course it does! And I'm certainly not saying there are only a handful of companies left in the world that ignore harassment. There are still plenty of backward companies out there. A California woman who worked as a physician's assistant at Sacramento's Mercy General Hospital was awarded $168 million dollars (the largest award to date) by a jury after it was proven that the hospital's HR department deliberately ignored her complaints about sexual harassment by surgeons and then terminated her employment. Sadly, many, many organizations have cultures that tolerate, or ignore, or sometimes even encourage harassment. In my opinion, those that do should be sued, preferably in class-action lawsuits, and have their leadership held personally accountable.

But I'm also saying that in the past few decades a lot of good companies with good, decent people running them have been besieged by countless harassment and discrimination lawsuits and extorted for six or seven figure settlements by disgruntled employees and their lawyers. Some of my clients and their insurers tell me that they consider these employment lawsuits and cash settlements to simply be part of the normal cost of business.

As a manager or supervisor, you must be aware, especially when it comes to inappropriate, prohibited or illegal behavior – stuff that gets people fired or lands them in court. So do yourself a big favor: become very familiar with your company's policies, procedures and resources on harassment. If you have questions, call HR or legal, or ask a manager with more experience. Also, you should know that there are many state and federal government agencies, like the EEOC, that are authorized to advise you, or at least receive a complaint.

By the way, if perchance you are engaging in inappropriate, offensive or illegal behavior yourself (and that includes everything from telling racy jokes and using foul language to surfing porn sites and sending offensive e-mail on company computers), I strongly recommend you stop immediately. Given all the media attention on harassment, there's a good possibility you will be caught and terminated. In 2001, for example, the US Navy terminated more than 300 contractors for e-mailing offensive jokes and pornographic photos to each other.

In addition to looking in your company's harassment policy, there's another place to go to figure out whether something is considered appropriate or not. That place is **your gut**. If your gut tells you something is offensive or inappropriate, it probably is. I'm convinced that most of us are not ax-murderers or psychopaths who can't tell the difference between right and wrong. Most of us are good, decent people who really do know if and when we are doing something wrong or offending someone. For example most everyone knows – even if they are from a foreign country with much looser harassment laws – that groping people, or making lewd, sexual remarks at work is totally inappropriate. No one needs a list to tell us this.

But, you ask incredulously, if everyone knows in their heart what's considered inappropriate language and behavior, why do people still do it? Excellent question. From what the psychologists tell us, people still do it for lots of different reasons. Some people...

- think they're better than others and don't have to play by the rules;

- refuse to admit, even to themselves, that they're doing something wrong;

- do it to get a "rise" out of others – to see if they can get others mad or upset;

- do it to test limitations and challenge the rules with which they don't agree – as teenagers do with their parents;

- think they can get away with it because it's perceived as common behavior – "Everybody does it!" (How many times have you heard that one?)

- are into power/head games and controlling others;

- continue to do it because no one has ever said anything to them about their bad behavior, so they have no idea that what they are doing is prohibited.

Whatever the personal justification, harassment still occurs in all forms, shapes and sizes. As a manager, it's your responsibility to avoid engaging in harassment and to really know your company's policies about it. Don't forget to trust your gut – it'll let you know if something's inappropriate. When it does, make sure to report it and document it.

Zero Tolerance vs. The Two Strike Rule. During the 1990's after being slammed with lawsuit after lawsuit, many organizations, including non-profits, instituted "zero-tolerance" policies on harassment. In brief, zero-tolerance means any – and I mean *any* – complaint about any behavior which is not related to work will be immediately and thoroughly investigated. Under such policies, anyone found to have engaged in inappropriate, offensive or illegal behavior will be subject to disciplinary action up to and including termination. Some organizations have set up 1-800 hot lines to accept harassment complaints anonymously, and trained legions of HR people in harassment investigation techniques, and are suspending and/or terminating employees for minor offenses to demonstrate how tough they are.

On paper "zero tolerance" appears to be all well and good; sending a blunt message that the organization is drawing a deep and clear line in the sand. In reality unfortunately, I believe there are many organizations – such a public schools – that are being overzealous in their interpretation of their zero tolerance policy. And I have heard of managers misinterpreting the policy and terminating employees for relatively minor infractions.

I've also been told about groups of employees who, having decided they don't like a particular manager for whatever reason, flood the 1-800 hot lines with false complaints about that manager. The result: managers who are constantly under investigation, their every sentence and move scrutinized and interpreted by earnest (and sometimes badly trained) investigators. And I've heard anecdotal evidence of good people being fired or hounded out of companies because of zero tolerance policies inappropriately or overzealously applied.

In my opinion, companies that zealously and publicly enforce zero tolerance policies assume that employees don't know right from wrong; that they can't be trusted to behave in a mature, responsible manner, and that they do not know how to resolve their conflicts for themselves. In such companies, I believe that zero tolerance becomes a self-fulfilling prophecy. I am convinced that like breeds like: employees who are not respected by their companies will end up treating each other with disrespect. Now who the heck wants to work in a place like this?

I have always maintained that there is a better, more respectful, more mature approach to workplace harassment which I call "The Two Strike Rule." In a nutshell, The Two Strike Rule gives each person one chance to be a complete jerk without automatically triggering a formal investigation and disciplinary process. Here's how it works. One day while at work, you decide to tell this offensive but (in your opinion) very funny joke to a bunch of your pals. Most of them laugh, but they also give you that look that let's you know you've been a bad boy or girl - you crossed over the line. You even knew before you told the joke that it was naughty, but you did it anyway.

Then someone has the personal fortitude to take you aside and tell you they were really offended by the joke (maybe they even use the "Straight Talk" tool on you!) You are mortified; you didn't mean to offend them, and you apologize profusely and sincerely, swearing you'll never do anything like it again. You also realize that this is your first strike. And you avoid telling jokes like this again, for a long, long time.

But then, one day, you slip and tell another offensive joke. This is "strike two," and unfortunately for you, it's time for a formal investigation and appropriate disciplinary action.

Now, when I advise a client to consider taking on The Two Strike Rule, I make it absolutely clear that it's an optional policy because anyone can and should feel free to report any kind of inappropriate behavior at any time and they should expect their organization to take the complaint seriously. In order to protect itself, every organization should investigate every complaint in some fashion.

But unlike zero tolerance, The Two Strike Rule allows a company to be more flexible, to make a determination that a full and formal investigation and disciplinary action need not be initiated after the first complaint, especially if the behavior, like telling an offensive joke, is not terribly egregious.

In my opinion, The Two Strike Rule gives employees the benefit of the doubt. It empowers them to see the error of their ways without a sword of Damocles hanging over their heads; and it encourages people to talk with each other, to let each other know when they've been offended.

Standard of Expected Behavior. In the old days, there used to be a standard of expected behavior on harassment that went something like this: *"If you wouldn't want it done to your wife, mother, sister or daughter, don't do it."* Now, at first glance this might seem like a common-sense, easy-to-understand standard. But I have a lot of problems with it. First of all, it's subjective. It assumes that all women are offended by the same things. Secondly, it assumes that only women are the targets of harassment, which we all know is just not true. And lastly, it's a sexist standard, implying that men know best as to how women should be treated. Frankly, I think this standard is a load of horse manure, and I do not recommend that any organization use it.

The standard I do recommend is called "The Media Standard" which is usually outlined like this: *"If you wouldn't want to see your name linked to negative behaviors in the newspaper or on the TV news, then don't engage in those behaviors."* In other words, if you wouldn't want to see your name in the local paper next to a description of groping, or violence, or flashing, or foul, abusive language, then don't do it. This Media Standard is an objective standard, it applies to all of us regardless of gender and I strongly recommend that organizations use it.

Lastly, as I've said again and again, if you are a manager or supervisor, you should personally document each and every incident you see or report. A detailed diary entry, or "memo-to-file" will do. In many companies the practice of documenting incidents is commonly and rather coarsely referred to as *"covering your butt."* But coarse or not, if you ever have to testify or defend yourself in court, you'll be very glad you did.

Primer 5

Leadership

Am I a manager or a leader, or both?

Real leaders keep their cool. A few days after the attacks on the World Trade Center and the Pentagon, I got a first hand look at a real leader in action, and was I ever impressed. What did this leader – a captain in the US Navy - do? He kept his cool in front of his team, even though world events and government bureaucrats were suddenly and unexpectedly threatening to dismantle everything he had been working on for a very long time.

I'd been advising this particular captain, who heads up a large technical group within the US Navy, on organizational change and teamwork issues.   For security reasons, I can't tell you more about who he is or what his group does. But I can say their work plays a key role in almost every combat branch of the US armed forces.

For six months this captain and his group had been gearing up for a major reorganization. They'd been holding strategic planning sessions, redefining their mission and vision statements, communicating constantly and generally doing all the right things to get ready for big, blockbuster-sized, change.

Then, the attacks of September 11th shocked the nation, and suddenly we were at war with terrorism. The top brass in Washington DC started rethinking everything the US military was doing, including the technical groups. And about a week later, just minutes before kicking off an all-hands meeting to publicly announce the names of the new leaders of his new organization, the captain got a cell phone call from Washington: "Hold it," he was told, "don't change anything."

Now, you can only imagine how he was feeling when he walked into the meeting after getting that call. And to be honest, not one of us there would have blamed him if he'd cussed and spit like a sailor. But he didn't do that. He took a deep breath, smiled and simply said that we'd hit a very major bump in the road. He didn't denigrate the problem or make light of it. He didn't curse the bureaucrats, the terrorists or fate. He calmly reminded us we were at war, and asked us to figure out – as a team – a way to work within uncertainty and move forward on all options.

How did we react? Well of course we were shocked, at first. I'm sure every person in that room was thinking, "There goes six months of hard work down the drain."

But, as the captain spoke from his heart about his personal commitment to helping our service men and women do their jobs in this time of war, our shock quickly transformed into determination. He reminded us that all of our meetings and planning were not a waste of time because we had become a tight, cohesive group in the process. And within minutes, I watched a group of 25 military personnel and civilian experts turn on a dime. Real leaders keep their cool when others around them are losing theirs.

The way I see it, the essential difference between a manager and a leader is this: a good manager has learned the tools and skills needed to manage projects and oversee the work of diverse groups of people. But good leaders go further and do more. Leaders, regardless of whether or not they are managers, actively develop their "emotional intelligence" throughout the course of their lives. They really walk the talk on taking care of and serving the people who work for them.

The concept of "emotional intelligence" was first developed during the 1980's by Peter Salovey of Yale University & John Mayer of the University of New Hampshire. They defined emotional intelligence as:

"The ability to monitor one's own and others' feelings and emotions, to discriminate among them, and to use this information to guide one's thinking and action."

During the 1990's, Daniel Goleman, who holds a Ph.D. from Harvard University, and who was a former senior editor of the periodical *Psychology Today,* generated enormous interest in emotional intelligence as a result of his books on the topic including, *Emotional Intelligence* and *Working With Emotional Intelligence.* I strongly recommend you read them and any other works you find on the subject.

Unlike your I.Q. (Intelligence Quotient), which is a numerical measurement of pure brain power and which supposedly remains the same throughout your life, emotional intelligence (EI) is something which can be developed and enhanced over the course of a lifetime.

According to Goleman and other experts, key emotional intelligence abilities are:

- Knowing your feelings and using them to make life decisions with which you can live;

- Being able to manage your emotional life without being hijacked by it — not being paralyzed by anxiety or worry, or swept away by anger;

- Persisting in the face of setbacks and channeling your impulses in order to pursue your goals;

- Empathy — reading other people's emotions without their having to tell you what they are feeling;

- Handling feelings in relationships with skill and harmony – for example, being able to articulate the unspoken pulse of a group;

Obviously you won't find these abilities listed in the average manager's job description.   These are complex self-knowledge and interpersonal – some cynics would say "warm and fuzzy" – skills and abilities that we expect to find in crisis counselors, ministers, battle-scarred military leaders, movie directors, police officers, social workers and therapists who have learned them after years of first-hand experience in the trenches of life.

Nevertheless, Goleman and his colleagues are convinced, as am I, that learning about and actively developing your emotional intelligence will result in your being considered a leader, regardless of whether or not you are a manager. At the risk of seeming self-congratulatory, I suggest that in buying this book, really reading it and practicing the tools within it, your are taking clear steps forward on the lifelong path of developing your emotional intelligence. There are many, many other ways to develop your emotional intelligence, including:

- When you learn about EI and analyze your own behavior in an EI context;
- As you mature, gain work/life experience, take risks and make mistakes;
- When you are challenged professionally/personally;
- When you observe and/or are mentored/coached by someone with a more developed EI, and you put what you've learned from them into practice yourself;
- When you have a significant personal event in which you experience a powerful insight (an "Ah Hah!").

Here are some typical situations in which your EI might develop:

- Declaring your love for another/having your heart broken;
- Receiving public acknowledgment/humiliation (i.e. award, pat-on-the-back, dressing down by boss, abuse);
- Responding heroically or running away in a crisis/emergency; (i.e. risking yourself to help a victim of car crash or fire);
- Doing the right/wrong thing on a difficult work challenge (i.e. taking a major business risk; standing up to inappropriate behavior; admitting a big mistake; shredding incriminating documents; blowing the whistle, etc.)

I think the best thing about emotional intelligence is that once you learn about it, and look at yourself within an EI context, you will never unlearn what you know and you will consciously and sub-consciously always try to develop your emotional intelligence until the day you die. As I said, developing your emotional intelligence is a practice that will make you a good leader.

Mentoring. Great leaders will often credit some of their success to the mentoring they received when they were younger, or new to their organization. A good mentor is someone who will generally look out for you in shark-infested corporate waters. The best mentor is someone in senior management or in an influential position who will be a sounding board for you, who can give you guidance, advice, coaching and who can open doors for you and positively influence others on your behalf. Good mentors will call you on your bad behavior, help you develop a workable career plan, and help you develop an exit strategy, just in case.

Many companies have formal mentoring programs in place, and they often work wonders for the people being mentored. But this usually depends on the mentors committing the time it takes to do it properly, and having enough clout and authority to open doors.

Where do you find a mentor if your company doesn't have a mentoring program? I've already mentioned a few times in this book that whenever you're in doubt about something, seek the advice and counsel of a more experienced manager. Surely you know at least one. And this person might be a good mentor for you. Or they will recommend someone else who might be better suited. Occasionally, your boss can be an excellent mentor. But usually, they are too close to you and the work you're doing together to be objective. There are also likely to be things you'd tell your mentor, but you'd never tell your boss.

The actual mentoring process varies from organization to organization, but it usually involves regular monthly or bi-monthly meetings in which you and your mentor go over your career development plan and address any problems or challenges you're currently facing. Together, you'll also identify good opportunities for you to meet other influential people in the organization and take on specific projects or tasks which will give you the chance to shine or excel. A number of tools we offer in this book including the modified "Coaching Your Colleague, " (page 75) and "Transition Coaching," (page 82) can be very useful to mentors and mentees.

Testing Yourself On Leadership. The following is a brief three-part self-assessment tool that I've developed for my training programs on leadership. It's similar in scope and theme to leadership/emotional intelligence assessments used by Goleman and other experts. Take it and consider the results to be a "snapshot" of where you are now on your understanding of leadership and of your potential to be a good leader.

I recommend you take it using a pencil, erasing your answers once you're done with the test. You may want to take it again in a year or so, to see how you've progressed. Lastly, this test is for your use only. I would advise against showing the results to anyone, because they really aren't useful to anyone but you.

PART ONE: Evaluating my understanding of leadership

For each of the statements below, mark whether you think the statement is true or false using a T for true or an F for false. Scoring found on page 64.

____ 1. The difference between a manager and a leader is good managers know how to organize, delegate, oversee and follow up, whereas good leaders know how to inspire, encourage and enable others.

____ 2. Leadership requires knowing what to communicate, when to communicate and how to communicate.

____ 3. Anyone can learn to be a good manager but only a very few people can learn to be good leaders.

____ 4. It's possible for leaders to emerge quickly; it doesn't take years of experience.

____ 5. Leaders help people generate ideas and take action on them.

____ 6. It's easy to spot a great leader.

____ 7. You have to plan and train for years to become a great leader.

____ 8. It is always the tough situations that bring out great leaders.

___ 9. Leaders generate a plan and enroll others into taking ownership of the details.

___ 10. The ability to command and control people is the most important quality of a great leader.

PART TWO: Evaluating my leadership behavior

For each of the statements below, record a 2 (Rarely), 4 (Seldom), 6 (Sometimes), 8 (Often), or 10 (Usually) in the blank for the number that corresponds with how often you engage in the behavior described. Scoring found on page 64.

I avoid telling people what to do. ___

In meetings, I listen as much as, if not more than I talk. ___

I try to consider other possibilities for action, even when they seem ridiculous. ___

I openly admit mistakes and apologize for them. ___

I make an effort to learn more about the people with whom I work. ___

I consider other viewpoints, even if I totally disagree with what they are. ___

I take time to walk around and "check in" with people, see how they're doing. ___

I look for the good in people and situations, rather than the negative. ___

I avoid complaining about people, things and situations. ___

I show a genuine interest in others and compliment their success. ___

I'll pitch in when needed, without complaint, even if I'm already overloaded. ___

I say "no" to requests when I have to, but I add, "here's what I can do." ___

I have a sense of humor and can laugh at myself. ___

I complete assignments/projects with full integrity, even if no one will know whether I have or not. ___

I refuse to tolerate disrespect and I treat others with respect. ___

I regularly communicate my goals and ideas using a variety of methods such as e-mail, phone, written memos/notes and face-to-face. ___

I look for the "big picture" in situations and for others to do so. ___

I plan ahead, trying to anticipate all possible events/reactions that might result from a specific action. ___

I occasionally stay late, come in early and/or work on weekends to get things done. ___

I surprise the people I work with a gift, card or personal note now and then. ___

I take care to articulate my thoughts and ideas, using metaphors, comparisons, catch-phrases and verbal illustrations to get things across to others as best I can. ___

I criticize constructively and coach others to generate new ideas and ways of solving problems. ___

I am passionate about what I'm saying or doing and I encourage others to be passionate too. ___

I encourage others to take care of themselves, take breaks, and to take time for personal issues if needed. ___

I follow through on my commitments. ___

I clearly communicate my vision and big picture ideas with others. ___

I'm flexible with others, finding ways to accommodate their needs. ___

I live up to my own standards of performance. ___

I seek out and leverage the diversity of experiences, skills and ideas in my work group. ___

If I were to ask the people I work with to answer these questions about me, they would select the same responses I did. ___

TOTAL   _____

PART THREE: Evaluating my own emotional intelligence

Circle the letter that best describes what you would do when faced with the given problem. Try to be as honest as you can as to how you would act. Remember, this is a self-assessment survey. Choosing the answer that you think the experts want you to choose will not tell you anything about yourself. Scoring found on page 64.

1. You're leading a meeting when you get the sense that one person is, or a number of people are suddenly acting differently than usual – either physically or verbally. What do you do?

    a.   Stop everything, and politely ask, "Is it something I said?"

    b.   Stop everything, and say, "I'm sensing something is up here; can some-one say what it is?"

    c.   Wait a little, try to figure it out on your own. If after a few moments, there are still negative feelings, then go to option b.

d.   Ignore it and keep moving. Given all you have to do, there isn't time to get bogged down with vague feelings.

2. Imagine you're a manager and you've asked a team you know well to work together on a project. After a few weeks, it becomes clear there are some major clashes going on with the team leader you picked and one or two of the others. What do you do?

a.   Stay out of it — let them deal with it on their own – they're all adults.

b.   Take the team leader aside and tell them point blank that they are responsible for the success of the team. Tell them to learn how to work better with the team, or they won't be leading the team in the future.

c.   Talk to some of the team members, see what they think the problem is.

d.   Tell them all together that you're disappointed with them, and then demote the leader and put someone else in the slot.

e.   Observe the team dynamics more, then coach the leader in private.

3. Imagine you're a graduate student who had hoped to get an A in a particular course, but you have just found out you got a C- on the midterm. What do you do?

a.   Create a specific plan for ways to improve your grade and actively follow through on your plans.

b.   Promise yourself you'll do better in the future.

c.   Remind yourself that it really doesn't matter much how well you do in any given test, it's the overall GPA that matters.

d.   Concentrate instead on the other classes where your grades are higher.

e.   Go to the professor privately and explain why you deserve a better grade.

4. Imagine you sell financial planning services and you make cold calls to many people every day. Today, nearly twenty people in a row have hung up on you, and you're getting discouraged. What do you do?

a.   Stop for the day and hope for better luck tomorrow.

b.   Take a look at yourself and figure out those things that may be undermining your ability to make a sale.

c.   Try something new in the next call, and keep trying.

d.   Consider quitting and doing something esle.

5. You're a manager who believes that it's important to encourage respect for other people's feelings. You also know how vital it is that people get along well with each other and that they find ways to bond. Today, you overhear someone in another department telling a joke that some people might find offensive. What do you do?

    a.   Ignore it — it's only a joke, and anyway, it's not your department.

    b.   Take the person aside and reprimand them in private.

    c.   Speak up on the spot to the entire group, saying that such jokes are inappropriate and will not be tolerated.

    d.   Interrupt and suggest to the person telling the joke that they go through a harassment training program.

6. You're in a high-level meeting with clients and colleagues. One of the clients makes a cutting, degrading and offensive remark about you and your inability to do the job properly. Now you're seething with rage. What do you do?

    a.   Tell yourself to forget it – that person is an idiot. Besides, s/he is a client, and can say whatever they want.

    b.   Ask them to step out of the room for a moment and let them know point blank that you will never ever allow them to speak like that to you again.

    c.   Avoid responding to the remark, or any remarks like it, during the meeting. Once the meeting is done, sit down in private with your colleagues and devise a response and plan of action.

    d.   Make a cutting, derogatory comment of your own right back at them.

7. You and one of your closest colleagues have gotten into an argument that has become a shouting match; you're both upset and making personal attacks based on things that you know about each other from years of experience. What's the best thing to do?

    a.   Take a break and then continue with the discussion.

    b.   Stop talking and don't say a word, no matter what your colleague says.

    c.   Say you're sorry and ask your colleague to apologize, too.

    d.   Stop, take a breath, then state your side of the case as accurately as you can.

8. You're a government manager who has been asked to lead a team that is trying to come up with a creative solution to an ongoing problem within your team/department/division/agency. What's the first thing you do?

    a. Schedule a meeting, then create a list of your ideas. During the meeting, go through each of your ideas and get feedback.

    b. When you first meet, do a quick "ice-breaker" so everyone can get to know each other better.

    c. Don't meet; instead conduct private interviews with each person get their ideas about how to solve the problem.

    d. Have a meeting, state the problem clearly and jump into a brainstorming session, encouraging everyone to say whatever comes to mind, no matter how wild.

9. A brand new employee has just joined a team that you lead. S/he seems extremely timid when interacting with everyone else. What do you do?

    a. Accept that the new person is shy and try to protect him/her from the more aggressive personalities on the team.

    b. Recommend s/he take an "interpersonal communication" course, or go to see a counselor, therapist or industrial psychologist who can help him/her come out of their shell.

    c. You don't have time for hand-holding. S/he is an adult, and is going to have to sink or learn to swim on their own.

    d. Take him/her aside, talk about your observations, work with them to develop a strategy for him/her to feel more comfortable with the team.

10. For years you've been bugging your manager to give you more responsibility for difficult tasks. One day, your manager calls you in to his/her office and says, "Okay, you asked for it." Then gives you a very complex task that is totally unlike anything you've done before. What do you do?

    a. Thank your manager gratefully, leave the office and then panic. Go to everyone you know and ask for help.

    b. Apologize and turn the task down, you know you're going to blow it.

    c. Ask your manager to coach you on generating a strategy for tackling the task and schedule some follow-up and check-in meetings to look over your progress.

    d. Tell your manager you've never done anything like this, and ask that s/he tell you how to do it. Tell him/her you don't want to let them down.

The Private Interview

Another way to assess your current level of leadership ability is to enlist the help of a bystander. Find a trusted colleague who knows you and your work. This could be your mentor if you have one. Then, request one hour for a private and confidential "professional development" meeting. Ask your colleague to answer your questions in an honest, mature and considerate manner. Remind him/her that you are doing this as part of your ongoing professional development. Then "interview your colleague" by asking the following questions. (Write the answers on a separate piece of paper.)

1. What do you consider to be my strengths as a manager?

2. What do you consider to be my weaknesses?

3. Is there anything you believe needs to be said to me that you, or others you know of, have not been able to say?

4. Is there anything for which you would like me to acknowledge you?

5. Is there anything for which you believe others would like me to acknowledge them?

6. Have I ever disappointed you or let you down?

7. Is there anything you, or others you know of, want to know from me?

8. If you could "adjust" me as a manager, what would you focus on?

Lastly, thank the trusted colleague for his or her time, candor and consideration.

Reviewing your findings: The Private Interview

Answer the following questions, specifically, on a separate sheet.

* By doing the Private Interview I learned...

• As a result, I'm resolved to ...

• I will begin doing these things on...

SCORING

PART ONE: Evaluating my understanding of leadership

1. T   6. F
2. T   7. F
3. F   8. F
4. T   9. T
5. T   10. F

PART TWO: Evaluating my leadership behavior
If your total score is...

242 – 300 Congratulations, you are a good leader. Keep growing.

182 – 240 You have a lot of what it takes to be a good leader, but need to engage more often in the types of behaviors listed.

122 – 180 You are not engaging enough in the types of behaviors listed in this section to be considered a leader. You could become a leader, but it will take work and personal commitment to change your behaviors and take on new ones.

60 – 118 You probably don't consider yourself a leader, nor is it likely that you want to be considered a leader.

PART THREE: Evaluating my own emotional intelligence

1. A=10, B=20, C=20, D=0. Choosing D reflects a lack of awareness of individual and group dynamics.

2. A=0, B=0, C=0, D=0, E=20. Emotionally intelligent managers take time to observe and learn before taking definitive action. Often the first step is to privately coach the team leader who is having trouble.

3. A=20, B=0, C=0, D=0. Being able to create a specific plan for overcoming obstacles and frustrations and following through on it is part of having a high level of emotional intelligence.

4. A=0, B=0, C=20, D=0. Staying positive in the face of disappointment is a sign of emotional intelligence. See problems as challenges you can learn from, and persist by trying out new ways of doing things instead of giving up, blaming yourself, or getting demoralized.

5. A=0, B=10, C=20, D=0. C is best, although B is a reasonable second choice. As a manager, people are always looking to you to set the tone. If you ignore inappropriate behavior, it will continue. Nevertheless, publicly reprimanding an individual or group can sometimes do as much or more damage than the initial inappropriate behavior. So, be careful.

6. A=0, B=0, C=20, D=0. When people make derogatory and cutting remarks to you in a public setting like a meeting, they are usually trying to bait you into an emotional outburst, and may try to use that outburst against you and your company in the future. Keep yourself under control in such circumstances, and then immediately discuss it in private with your colleagues and develop an appropriate response/strategy.

7. A=20, B=0, C=5, D=0. Take a break of 20 minutes or more. This allows your body the time to clear itself of the physiological results of being angry. Anger can distort your perception. After a break, you'll both be more likely to have a fruitful discussion.

8. A=0, B=20, C=0, D=5. Groups work best when their rapport and comfort levels are high. Even groups who have worked together for years can benefit from an ice-breaker just to get them to see old relationships in a new way. Sometimes, there's simply no time to do one, so answer D is the next best choice.

9. A=0, B=5, C=0, D=20. Everyone is different and responds differently to new people and situations. Even the shyest people can make valuable contributions, if you have a strategy to capture them.

10. A=0, B=0, C=20, D=0. Being honest about your limitations and asking for help are key indicators of emotional intelligence.

Results/Assessments:

140 – 200 Pts. You have a very high emotional intelligence level and are well suited for leadership right now.

90 – 135 Pts.   You have achieved a medium to high level of emotional intelligence. If you continue learning about yourself and further develop your skills and understanding of human nature, you will be well positioned for leadership.

50 – 85 Pts.   Your emotional intelligence is at a fairly low level. It's likely you are having trouble understanding how your behavior impacts others and you are insensitive to others needs and feelings.

0 – 45 Pts.   Your emotional intelligence is entirely undeveloped. It's likely you prefer to work alone, you avoid conflict and taking risks. To become a true leader, you would need training, self-examination and experience.

Tools

The following tools provide options for dealing with bad behavior, people problems and sticky situations. I recommend you look over each of them two or three times to ensure they make sense to you. I also suggest you compare and contrast them with other manager's tools you've used before or have been exposed to in your career. You may find that these are better than, or not as good, as the ones you already use.

No tool fits every situation perfectly, for example, when trying to get someone to cut back on their use of foul language, "Classic Straight Talk" (page 74) may be too harsh and formal. You may want to soften or modify it to suit the situation/mood. Or you may want to use "The Sandwich Technique." In other words, these tools aren't written in stone. Adapt or combine them as you see fit.

Lastly, as I've said before, please try to practice using these tools with a trusted colleague or friend before using them in real life. Without practice, you could make a bad situation much worse.

The 2-Minute REDIRECT

Use: The 2-minute REDIRECT tool is used as a nonthreatening way to challenge team members to perform better, without pulling them away from their work.

STEPS

Describe: What you've observed in neutral terms, "This is what I see..."

Interval: Allow an interval of time to listen and wait for their response.

Remind: Remind them of what you expect them to do.

Clear: Come to a clear agreement on what happens next.

Timeline: Make a timeline for when to check in with each other.

Typical example:

You've found one of your employees has made some calculation errors.

You: "Hi, (name), it looks to me that there may be some errors in here. What do you think?"

Them: "Could be, I'm not sure. I thought I was doing it right."

You: "Well, it's always a good idea to check your work a few extra times before handing it in. Why don't you take a look at this again?

Them: "Okay."

You: "I'll come back later on, to see how it's going. Thanks."

The 60-Minute Mediation

Use: The 60-Minute Mediation is used to bring together two team members who have trouble working together. The mediation will assist them in moving forward positively and productively.

STEPS

1. *Level of Seriousness.* Determine if the behavior of either individual warrants a more formal report or investigation by designated individuals (HR, legal). If not...

2. *Create an "End State Statement.* Determine the problem as you perceive it. Then develop a business case focused "End State Statement" for yourself in which the problem is no longer a factor (page 77).

3. *Advance One-on-One Meetings.* If possible, arrange to meet in advance with each individual to get his or her take on the problem.   Advise each one that you will bring them together in a mediation meeting. Warn them of the consequences of not participating in the mediation meeting and process.

4. *Private Meeting Site.* Bring the two parties together in a private location (your office or a secure conference room) or off-site entirely (coffee shop or park).

5. *Impact/Overview of Your Problem.* State the problem as you perceive it, including its impact on you, the individuals involved, and the team. Tell them you are here to ask them to work out ways to move forward. Reminder: you're a <u>mediator, not an arbitrator.</u>

6. *Ground Rules.*
   • Each person may present his or her version of events <u>without interruption.</u>
   • They should state what happened, not their interpretation of what happened.
   • Treat each other respectfully at all times.
   • We will work out discrepancies in "the facts" as we go.
   • By the end of the meeting, we will have devised and mutually agreed on a strategy and timeline for moving forward positively and productively.

7. *Commonalities.* After each has stated his or her case, look for positive things they agree upon, even if they are basic. For example, "You both want to work within a team without a lot of tension, right?"

8. *Clean Up & Acknowledgment.* Coach each to offer an unqualified apology on some aspect of the problem for which they are responsible.

continued, next page...

The 60-Minute Mediation, continued...

9. *Mediate a Strategy.* Ask one or both to generate an "action-item based strategy" for moving forward. Get a response to the strategy from the other. Seek mutual agreement on the action items in the strategy and timeline involved. Remind them of your "End State Statement" periodically throughout the process. Remind them of the impact of not living up to their agreement.

The "Changed Man" Technique

Use: The "Changed Man" Technique is to be used by a manager who has engaged in inappropriate or offensive behavior and been ostracized by staff and colleagues for it. The technique will help to "free" the manager from the stigma and allow him or her to positively and constructively move forward in the organization.

Two years ago, this technique was used by a principal of an international management consulting group who had been accused of having adulterous affairs with colleagues, been seen drinking excessively with subordinates after work nightly, and been arrested for DWI. After using the "Changed Man" Technique, the individual is now a major player with the firm, does not engage in those behaviors, and is considered an ethical leader by colleagues.

STEPS

1. While working with a private, confidential coach, the manager should make a very detailed list of offensive behavior AND other behaviors that he or she is willing to change once and for all. The other behaviors do not need to be major problems– in fact it helps if they are not. They should be little but noticeable things (biting nails, arriving late to work, messy desk). Then, add new, good behaviors to the list (clean desk, arrive on time). The manager should tell no one except the private coach about this list.

2. If there has been a public "outing" of the manager's behavior, approximately 1-2 weeks after the event, the manager announces to an assistant or colleague that he or she will be taking time off (approximately 3-5 business days) to go out of town to attend a "personal development seminar." If asked for specifics, the manager should respond sincerely by saying, "It's a closed-door off-site session for a small group. They've asked that no one be permitted to contact me unless it's a family emergency." Offer no more explanation.

Note: *During the period preceding the time off, the manager should wrap up any pressing business issues to make sure that no business emergency will arise while they are away from work. Designate a colleague to catch any business emergencies that do come up.*

3.   Approximately 1-2 days before the time off, the manager should remind assistant and one colleague that they are going away and that no one from work should contact him or her. No one should call the manager's home— make this crystal clear.

4.   The manager should not be seen or heard from for 3-5 business days. It is imperative that no one contacts the manager while he or she is gone. The manager should not respond to any contacts from work, including e-mail. Family should be instructed to take messages but make no guarantees that manager will respond.

5.   Although no one can force the manager, it is recommended that he or she does go away to attend some kind of personal development seminar (there are many good ones). Nevertheless during the time away from work, the manager should review the list they made in STEP 1 to the point where they can commit it to memory. The manager should also change their hairstyle (even just a little), go to a tanning salon, get as much rest as possible, and purchase one or two new outfits (clothes they wouldn't normally wear before). Practice the new behaviors again and again.

6.   The manager arrives back at work and has a "catchup" meeting with colleagues and support staff as necessary. They should say nothing about the time away, but immediately start practicing the new good behaviors. If anyone asks how the seminar went, the manager tells them "terrific" and leaves it at that.

7.   Continue the new good behaviors and NEVER engage in the old ones again. If anyone brings up the bad behaviors, tell them, "That was then. That's done."

The Decision Matrix

I consider this to be one of the most important and valuable tools in this book. Please don't make notes on the matrix in this book. Instead I recommend you make enlarged photocopies of it as needed.

Use: The Decision Matrix is a very practical tool for making decisions about how to handle or respond to bad behavior, people problems and sticky situations.

STEPS

Sit down and focus on the issue/situation. Work from the left column by column, moving down before you move to the next column to the right. At the end, document what action was taken and when. Record your responses in a photocopied version of the following Decision Matrix so that it can be used again and again.

COLUMN ONE. What am I trying to accomplish? List your specific goals in relation to the issue/conflict at hand. Be specific and list the major challenges you're facing in regard to these goals.

COLUMN TWO. What differences and diversity dimensions are involved? Is this decision related to race, gender, disability, ethnicity, work-life balance, religion, socio-economic status, age, sexual orientation, veteran status, generation, organizational status, seniority, personality, a combination of any of the above, or another differences/diversity dimension not listed?

COLUMN THREE. What are my options? What are all the options available to me? Are there any specific challenges that accompany these options?

COLUMN FOUR. What's the impact of the options on the business? What are the positive impacts on the business related to each option? What are the nega-tives?

COLUMN FIVE. How would I feel if it were me? How would I act/react/handle these options if I were the person(s) about whom a decision is going to be made? Would I want things done differently? What would be all my positive and negative reactions to the situation?

COLUMN SIX. What do I do? Write down an overview of what you intend to do. List related decisions.

The Decision Matrix

What is my goal or End State Statement?	What are "differences" and issues are involved?	What are the options?	What is the impact of each option on our business?	How would I feel if I was the person(s) at the center of the decision?	What do I do? What's my decision? What are the specific action items that result directly from my decision? When do they need to happen?
Specifics:	Specifics:	Specifics:	Positives:	Positives:	Overall decision:
Challenges:	Related issues:	Challenges to each:	Negatives:	Negatives:	Related decisions:

Classic Straight Talk*

Use: Classic Straight Talk is a face-to-face, on-the-spot tool to put an immediate halt to inappropriate, offensive, prohibited or illegal behavior. It's best to use this with someone without anyone overhearing. If they are in a group, for example, pull them aside out of earshot.

An easy way to remember this tool is to think of the actor Johnny DEPP and add a PC to the end.

STEPS

Describe:	Describe the behavior in neutral terms.
Effect:	Explain the effect of the behavior on you and the organization.
Pause:	Pause to gauge response. *(If they are denying that there's a problem, go back to the beginning, start again.)*
Prefer:	Describe the preferred behavior in the future.
Positive:	Give a positive remark about the individual.
Consequence:	If no sincere apology is offered, then explain the consequences of continuing inappropriate behavior.

D - "When people tell offensive jokes in the workplace..."

E - "It embarasses me that a member of my team would do this and it makes it look as if this is a place where people don't respect each other."

P - (pause)

P - "I'd prefer that you not tell jokes like that in the future."

P - "You're a good person. I'm sure we won't have to have a conversation like this again."

C - "If this happens again, we'll have to get involved with the harassment policy and procedures."

* This tool was taught to me by Gary Dichtenberg of Professional Development Associates in Atlanta, GA. Gary is an amazing person with a lot of experience and provides his clients with outstanding programs and services.

Coaching Your Colleague

Use: To give constructive coaching to a colleague about their personality and/or behavior.

Note: This technique is best used by someone who is close to the individual in question. Beforehand, decide specifically what area/issue you are going to address with them. Use a separate sheet to write down your thoughts prior to doing the coaching. Actual coaching time will take from 20-45 minutes.

1. *Private time?* Ask if you could have some private time with them to discuss some issues that have come up for you recently.

2. *I hope I can be helpful.* Tell them that your hope is they will find your observations useful and valuable.

3. *Acknowledge them.* Acknowledge them as a person/colleague by telling them about something specific which they did that you think is a good indicator of what a good person/colleague they are.

4. *Only my observations.* Acknowledge that what you are about to talk about are only your observations and perceptions, not necessarily "the truth."

5. *Describe behavior.* Describe the behavior that you observed in regard to the issue that concerns you most. Use neutral (non-blaming) language.

6. *How you perceived it.* Tell them how you perceived their behavior; how it impacted you and/or how you perceived it impacting others.

7. *Ask, "Am I making sense?"* Make sure they understand what it is you're talking about.

8. *Reassure them.* Make sure they know you don't think they intentionally meant harm/hurt/upset to you or others.

9. *Pause.* See if they want to talk about it; ask questions; etc. *NOTE: If they become "defensive/angry/deny" don't push back! Just reiterate, this is what I observed, this is how I perceived it.*

10. *Check in.* Even if their response is very favorable, ask, "Would you have preferred I not said anything?"

11. *Ask one more time.* "Is there anything (more) you want to ask or say to me about this?"

12. *Ask, "Have I helped?"* "Has this been helpful?" (If yes, respond with "I'm glad and thanks for listening." If no, just thank them for listening and for their time.)

Modified "Coaching Your Colleague"
(for use by mentors and coaches)

STEPS:

1. *20 Minutes.* Ask for 20 minutes of uninterrupted time.

2. *Open to Coaching?* Ask, "Are you open to coaching right now?" (If "no," ask them to vent about whatever they need to vent about. Give them one minute to vent.)

3. *Three Hottest Projects.* Ask, "What are your three hottest, most pressing projects/concerns/tasks right now?"

4. *Greatest Positive Impact.* Ask, "Which of these, when completed, will have the greatest positive impact on our organization?"

5. *What's Stopping You?* Ask, "What's stopping you from completing this project?"

6. *What Will Unstop You?* Ask, "What specifically will get you unstopped on this project?"

7. *When Will You Start?* Ask, "When are you going to start completing this project?"

8. *Can I Help?* Ask, "Is there anything I can do to help you?"

9. *Follow-up Date?* Ask "When will we be speaking again so I can follow up with you on this and other projects?"

10. *Thanks.* Thank them for being so "coachable."

The End State Statement (E.S.S.)

Use: To get yourself clear on how you want things to be in the future. The End State Statement is a snapshot of how you want things to be when a meeting, process, event or period of time is over.   It's especially useful to new managers who are engaging with a difficult individual or group. And it can be used when you are setting Clear Expectations (see F.A.C.T. in Primer Two, page 17) with employees.

Note: usually a typical E.S.S. contains realistic, attainable goals, but it can also be a very high, stretch goal designed to motivate others into action.

Questions to ask yourself to develop your E.S.S.
1. What specifically do I want to see when this is over and done?
2. When do I expect it to be completed?
3. What words can I use that will make the E.S.S. positive, clear and definitive?

Examples of good End State Statements:

"By the end of this trial period, you are fully trained and experienced on the responsibilities of this position, and are ready to teach someone else how to do it so you can be promoted."

"When I leave this division in two years, I want to see revenues increased by 50%, complaints at an all-time low, and turnover at 5%."

"When the month is over, you two will have settled your personal differences and found a positive and productive way of working together on this project."

"When this is all over, Richard is an enthusiastic and totally available resource to the e-commerce development team."

"Your report will be complete, error-free and on my desk by the end of the week."

"By 2005, my book will be on the desk of every manager in every Fortune 500 company."

H. E. A . R.

Use: This is a de-escalation technique to help you cool somebody (or a small group of people) down.

Halt: Halt what you are doing and focus on the speaker

Explore: Explore the problem by asking who, what, when, and how questions (avoid why). Continuously bring the discussion back to "How does this specifically impact our business/what we are doing?"

Acknowledge: Acknowledge the speaker's feelings and frustrations; use reflective listening ("I can see you're upset/worried/concerned about…").

Respond: Respond to the problem on the spot or determine a date on which you will respond. Ensure you do provide them with a response of some kind on the date you promised.

When doing the H.E.A.R. technique, remember to:

- Maintain eye contact, but don't stare.

- Avoid distractions.

- Face the speaker.

- Keep arms unfolded.

- Keep hands unclenched.

- Keep focused, be able to – at any moment- repeat back to the person, ver-batim, what they just said to you.

- Use reflective listening: paraphrase accurately without adding your spin.

- Ask the speaker for their ideas as to how to resolve the concern.

- Acknowledge their feelings without necessarily promising to fix the problem for them.

Manager's Straight Talk

Use: The Manager's Straight Talk is a face-to-face tool to provide a formal verbal and/or written warning to an employee about inappropriate behavior. It can be used to deliver your organization's normal and established reprimand.

Note: This process has been reviewed and approved by a number of attorneys who are experts in employment law.

STEPS

1. *Others Know.* Start the meeting by mentioning that you have received guidance from HR/Legal on how to proceed (after actually contacting HR/legal).

2. *Positive.* Tell the individual something positive about him or her related to work.

3. *Classic Straight Talk.* Do the "D" and "E" steps of "Classic Straight Talk" on page 74.

4. *Copies.* Provide a copy of relevant policies, procedures, letters, reports, etc.

5. *Questions?* Remind them to look through everything and to return to you with questions, if any.

6. *Retaliation.* Remind them that retaliation against anyone will not be tolerated.

7. *Equality.* Remind him or her that you'll be treating everyone on the team equally and expect a certain standard of behavior from everyone.

8. *Preferred Behavior.* Do the "P" (preferred) step of Classic Straight Talk and state a standard of expected behavior.

9. *Final Positive.* Finish up with an additional positive statement about the individual related to work or this meeting.

10. *Apology.* Wait for an apology. If none comes, remind them about consequences of continuing with the behavior.

11. *Document.* Document the meeting and report results to HR/legal.

The Sandwich Technique

Use: When someone mis-performs, give him or her a sandwich!*

STEPS

The soft top: "You do great work..."

The meat: "But on this project, there is a problem with x, y and z."

The soft bottom: "You're very flexible (or intelligent or quick); I am sure we won't have to address this again."

* Many of my colleagues, experts I respect, have concerns about this technique; because it seems to them to be disingenuous and/or a softening technique that undermines the direct feedback (the meat) that needs to be given. They also feel it could become a crutch that a manager comes to rely on so much that people "see it coming" and automatically devalue the direct feedback.   While I understand and, to a certain extent agree with their concerns, I still maintain that this tool has some value in certain situations, especially with new and/or less experienced employees who may lack the self-confidence and resilience to accept direct feedback without also being told they are good at other things.

Termination Meeting

Use: This technique is a step-by-step process for terminating an employee, which is always a difficult and potentially upsetting process for all parties. Before terminating any employee, it is imperative that you check with legal counsel to ensure you have appropriate and justifiable grounds for termination.

Note: This process has been reviewed and approved by a number of attorneys who are experts in employment law.

1. *Privacy.* Arrange for a meeting in a private place where the employee can leave afterward with the least amount of interaction with others – it is advisable to have a witness in the meeting. Ensure additional help/security is on standby nearby.

2. *Inform of termination.* Inform the employee of the company's decision to terminate within the first few minutes. This is not your decision alone, it is the company's.

3. *Present facts.* Present the facts as to why they are being terminated – no glossing over or phony excuses.

4. *Focus on performance.* Focus on his or her performance, not personality.

5. *Empathize.* Empathize while remaining firm.

6. *Allow for venting.* Allow him or her the opportunity to vent, but be prepared to call for help if the person becomes enraged or volatile.

7. *Severance.* Inform of all severance packages, final payments and carry-forward benefits, etc. Remind him or her that written materials on these will be sent in the mail soon.

8. *Reference.* Inform them of whether or not you can provide a reference (if not, say, "It would be better for all if we did not provide a reference").

9. *Exit interview.* Conduct an exit interview on the spot if appropriate or possible.

10. *Escort to work area.* Escort him or her to their work location to assist in collection of personal belongings and prevent them from taking or damaging company equipment and data.

11. *Escort off premises.* Escort him or her off the premises.

12. *Document.* Document the termination meeting clearly.

13. Send out severance materials.

14. Follow up with an exit interview in person or by mail if one was not done on the spot.

Transition Coaching

Use: Transition Coaching is used to help guide an individual through a career or work transition. It is best if a manager, supervisor, or someone close to the individual in question uses this technique. Beforehand check in with HR to determine if this course of action is in line with policy and procedure. Then create an End State Statement (E.S.S., page 77) and decide specifically what you believe the coachee should be doing, but never let them know what you've already decided. Choose a private, appropriate time and location for the coaching session. Avoid interruptions and allow time for reflective listening and personal reflection.

STEPS

1. *Open to coaching? Ask* them if they are open to coaching right now.

2. *Acknowledgment. Ac*knowledge them as a person/employee.

3. *Three negatives. Ask* them to name the top three most negative things about their work/job/situation.

4. *Three positives. Ask* them to name the top three most positive things about their work/job/situation.

5. *"Magic Wand" question. Ask,* "If you could wave a magic wand and change your work/job/situation right now, what would your new job/work/situation look like?"

6. *Considered doing something different?* Ask, "Have you considered doing X, Y, Z or taking the X, Y, Z job?"

7. *What could you do?* Ask, "What could you do to make that change actually happen?"

8. *What could we do?* Ask, "What could I and the organization do to make that change actually happen?"

9. *Get specific.* Clarify the steps required to enable the change to happen.

10. *What's the first step?* Ask, "What do you think is the first step you can take to start the process? When will you take that step?"

11. *Helpful?* Ask, "Has this been helpful?"

12. *Call anytime.* Remind them, "Call me anytime you need help or advice." Thank them for listening.

Follow up. Follow up with them very soon (report back to HR if necessary).

Verbal Agreement Contract

Use: This tool is used to establish agreement and mutual understanding between a manager and team member about a job or task. It's great for use on the spot.

STEPS

1. Job Statement A: Manager states, "This is the job as I see it..."

2. Job Statement B: Team member states, "This is the job as I understand it..."

3. Clear Agreement: Manager states the "agreement" they share, "So we agree that..."

4. Define the Time: Both agree on when the job is to be done.

Written Case Studies
(for use with The Decision Matrix)

The following case studies are based on actual events and situations that occurred within my clients' organizations. The real names of the people involved and the nature of their organization's work have been deliberately changed so that none of my clients will recognize themselves or their organizations.

I find many managers and supervisors have seen, heard about or will experience challenges similar to these at some point in their careers, so I'm convinced these case studies will resonate with you and be very useful to you.

Each case study treats you as the manager faced with particular bad behaviors, people problems and sticky situations. The case study describes your role, the background to the situation and the current problem you are facing. At the end of each case study, you are given a choice of actions to take and a chance to identify tools that you might use to move forward on those actions.

These case studies are designed to allow you to practice using The Decision Matrix. Now, because you're human, I assume you will read each case study and the possible solutions and then make a gut decision first, *without* using The Decision Matrix. I also assume you'll then skip ahead to find the answer in the "recommended approach" section so you can see how you've done. That's all right, you're forgiven.

However, after you've indulged yourself, I want you to take out the Decision Matrix and really use it on each case study. Using the Matrix, you may find that your gut was right on target. You may find that it misled you. But no matter what, you can at least say you went through a thoughtful, logical process of checking your gut reaction to a given situation. My hope is, you'll use the Decision Matrix enough times in this book and become so familiar with the process that you will automatically use it every time you are faced with bad behavior, people problems or sticky situations.

Directions. With a pencil, circle the letter of the choice that best describes what you would do if faced with a similar problem. Then in the lines provided, record what action you would take and tool(s) you would use to resolve the situation.

A recommended approach to each situation is located at the end of each section. Good luck!

CASE STUDIES: Bad Behavior

Body Odor

Role. You are the line manager for a group of engineers and technical folks that includes many foreign nationals.

Background. One of your direct reports is Cassie Akira, a Japanese-American woman from Los Angeles. She's a great engineer and very hard worker but she has a cynical, negative side to her that lately seems to dominate all interactions with you and others. These days it's rare that she has a nice thing to say about anyone or anything.

Cassie is a pal with a Chicago "wise-guy" on a project team she's assigned to, a real character named Brian Andrews. Brian is into off-color jokes and cynical remarks – typical Chicagoan as far as you can tell. Brian does not report to you.

Current Problem. This morning, Abdul, another engineer who reports to you, came in to make a complaint about Cassie and Brian. Abdul is from the United Arab Emirates and has been with your company for three years. He's a quiet man and an excellent engineer. There's never been a problem with Abdul.

According to Abdul, a few days ago, Cassie and Brian were in a break room heating food in a microwave when Abdul came in to get a drink from the vending machine. They were pleasant enough to him while he was there. He left the break room and started walking down the hall and then realized he had wanted a packet of chips for lunch. He headed back to the break room and just before he stepped in, he overheard Cassie saying, "Abdul has atrocious body odor." Brian agreed with her adding, "These Arabs are driving me nuts. It's either feast or famine with them." Cassie agreed, saying, "No kidding, we either have to smell their stinky food all the time, or we get no food in our meetings 'cause they're fasting for Ramadan or some other crazy holiday." Abdul says he then walked back in and got the chips. They immediately stopped talking. He is sure they knew he overheard them, but they pretended that everything was fine. What do you do?

A.   Tell Abdul that everyone has biases and says dumb things about others now and then. Since their comments were not supposed to be overheard by him, there's really nothing you can do about it. Tell him to get a thicker skin.

B.   Thank Abdul for coming to you about it. Tell him you will look into it and get back to him later. Let Brian's line manager know about the incident. Then speak with Cassie separately about her behavior.

C.   Tell Abdul you'll handle it and then during the next team meeting remind everyone about respecting each member of the team and valuing diversity.

D.   Tell Abdul to go talk to Cassie and Brian himself.

E.   A combination of the above, or another option altogether.

Tools you might use:

Burnout

Role.   You are a principal of a medium-sized consulting firm specializing in serving the technical/IT needs of major manufacturers. You're an engineer by training, education, experience and temperament.

Background.   Three years ago, your firm asked you to move yourself and your family to the Northwest to serve a new client and oversee the firm's growth in that marketplace. They offered to put you on partner track if you accepted. You agreed and moved your family shortly thereafter. You also asked a colleague at the firm, Keith, whom you've worked with for many years, to come with you. He and his wife agreed and since they had no children, the move did not seem as stressful for them as it was for you and your family.

You and Keith immediately hit the ground running. You were the "big picture" guy who won the new business and contracts, and Keith was the "nuts and bolts" guy who handled the clients and their staffing needs. This arrangement seemed to work well, for a while.

Current Problem.   Lately you are hearing a lot of complaints about junior staff feeling "stuck" with these manufacturing clients for the rest of their careers. Turnover among the junior staff is very high, but Keith keeps assuring you that everything will be okay and the clients aren't complaining. Besides, you don't like those manufacturing folks anyway and you're too busy building the business. Keith will figure it out, he always has.

But one day at a company outing to a ballgame, you notice Keith drinking a little too much and partying just a little too hard with the junior staff. And someone drops a rumor that Keith is "having an affair" with one of the married women on staff. In the weeks that followed the ballgame, you can't help observing that Keith is not coming in as early as he used to; he's missing more of his deadlines and complaints about him "schmoozing" the junior staff are piling up. You've also noticed that he's lost a lot of weight, has started smoking again and generally seems to be in a foul and unhappy mood.

So you go to him in private to see if you can help. Keith vehemently denies he's having an affair and says that that he's mostly overworked and stressed out. You aren't sure you believe what he's saying about the affair so you warn him about what might happen if it were true. You also encourage him to take the vacation he keeps putting off. He tells you it's really his wife who keeps putting it off because of money problems and that his home life is not good. Suddenly he seems about to burst into tears. You become very uncomfortable and suggest he take a vacation. He says he'll talk to his wife but he doesn't expect much from her. You get out of there as quickly as you can. You're really worried about Keith personally because you think he's depressed. But you're worried about the clients and the staff. What do you do?

A.   You find a private psychologist/therapist and order Keith to go. In the meantime, you take on his duties yourself and tell no one.

B.   You call a meeting with all the other senior staff and try to shift some of the work and responsibility away from Keith. You make sure you brief Keith before this meeting about what you're going to do, "to relieve some of the pressure," but you tell no one else what your motives are. You tell Keith he has no choice but to cooperate with what you're doing. And you continue to insist he take a vacation.

C.   You call HR right away and tell them they've got to get help for Keith. Let them handle it; they're the professionals. They may have to launch an investigation into the allegations about him having an affair, but that's too bad. If it's not true, then that'll be that. If it is true...well, you'll cross that bridge when you get to it.

D.   You investigate the allegations yourself, that's your responsibility and a way of protecting Keith's reputation. As far as his personal problems are concerned, that's none of your business, he'll have to sort it out on his own.

E.   Any combination of the above or another option altogether.

Tools you might use:

Customer Service

Role. You are a female supervisor in a customer service operation of a credit card company.

Background. Your group of 50 reps, comprised mostly of females and gay men, is responsible for responding to customer requests for information. They are on the phones 24/7, and due to high call volume, the place is usually just one notch short of total chaos. Nevertheless everyone seems to love working there. Up until a year ago, this was not the case. Turnover at that time was nearly 50% per quarter, and there were tons of complaints filed with HR. There were all sorts of backstabbing and political games being played within the group. On top of all this, customer satisfaction was low and management was holding you responsible for everything that was going wrong. Things could not have been worse.

Finally, after you complained day in and day out, management suddenly realized they were spending hundreds of thousands of dollars on legal fees and settlements as a result of this group and decided they needed to bring in a consultant to help. Fortunately, the consultant actually knew what s/he was doing and recommended sweeping changes after conducting a detailed assessment and focus groups. The changes included: dismantling the old setup of rows of gray cubicles and replacing it with open plan seating at round tables with clear glass privacy walls; replacing the fluorescent lights with full spectrum bulbs; allowing everyone to bring in plants and posters and other personal items; and introducing reward/compensation packages that encouraged the reps to support each other rather than undermine each other.

Now turnover has fallen to a manageable 10 percent, many of the employees are close friends, and the level of fun and camaraderie couldn't be higher. Plus, the level of lawsuits and complaints has dropped considerably.

Current Problem. You've noticed that lately things have gotten a little too cozy and familiar. For example, although the reps are still very professional with the customers on the phone, they tend to use foul or sexually explicit language with each other. They also talk a lot about their personal lives, their sex lives. A number of them even have bets on who is going to hook up with whom and how long the relationship might last. Quite a few butts are being pinched more frequently every day and there's a lot of racy language and laughter floating around the room. Someone brought in a Chippendales calendar and posted it next to the beverage dispensers.

Still you remember that customer satisfaction surveys are very high and no one in senior management ever says anything about the "fun" atmosphere of your group. In fact senior management is so happy, they haven't even bothered to come down here in months. Should you do/say anything?

A.   No point, if it ain't broke, don't fix it. No one is doing anything illegal and the group is performing very well. Wait for someone to clearly go over the line and then take action quickly and quietly.

B.   Issue or post a memo reminding everyone about the company's policy, procedures, and resources in regard to harassment and hostile work environment. This will cover you if anything does happen and protect the company too.

C.   At a group meeting, lay down the law, saying "things have gotten out of control and it needs to stop." Single out the folks who are engaging in the really outrageous behavior and put them on warning. Tell them you regret doing this but it's for everyone's benefit.

D.   Ask one of the more conservative senior managers to come by for a "surprise visit" just to rattle everybody a little bit. Tell them he wasn't pleased with what he saw and that he's holding you accountable. Regretfully inform them of all the behaviors that have to stop. Monitor compliance and discipline those who continue to engage in the inappropriate behavior.

E.   Get everyone together informally to discuss how the group dynamic may be affecting their ability to perform their jobs. Solicit suggestions as to how to improve it or change it. Listen closely and then implement their suggestions.

F.   Any combination of the above or another option entirely.

Tools you might use:

Strained Relations

Role. You are a newly appointed manager in a high-tech company.

Background. For the past few months you've noticed two staff members in the office have been very cold and distant with each other. They are Lydia Munoz and Jay Thomson. Their relationship is strained to say the least and it's beginning to impact office morale and the productivity of the team.

Current Problem. Today at a team meeting you asked Jay to pull some data, analyze it, and hand it off to Lydia when it was complete, so that she can use it in a report she is preparing. You asked him to get it to her on time by next Friday. As you were about to move on to other business, you heard Lydia make a quiet remark to the person sitting next to her. You weren't sure what she said, but you think it was "Is s/he kidding? There is no way he's going to get this to me on time." You noticed Jay was glaring at Lydia after she said this. As far as you're concerned, this is the straw that's broken the camel's back. It's time to get the problems between Lydia and Jay out on the table and handled, so you meet privately with each of them, Lydia first.

You told her you're seeing tension between her and Jay and you noticed her making comments about him. You asked specifically what her problem with Jay is. She replied that he's a "third wheel" who is impeding the group's forward momentum. She doesn't know why he's on the team or what he's supposed to be doing. You assured her he does have a role and that she had to learn to work with everyone on the team.

When Jay came in, you told him exactly the same things you said to Lydia. Jay said he didn't have any problems at all, that he enjoyed working with everyone and that he didn't see or perceive any of the problems that you did. He seemed sincere in his denials to the point where you doubted your own senses. But when you asked specifically about Lydia, you noticed that Jay stiffened up. He remarked that her style is typical of "people like her" and is to be expected. He said he wasn't bothered by it. At that point you didn't believe him and you mentioned the comment you overheard her make during the meeting. Jay claimed he didn't hear it clearly and shrugged it off. What do you do?

A. You call them both in for a meeting to ask them about it together. You tell them they need to find a way to work together and that you will assist them. You document the process and you develop a timetable for meetings to get it done.

B. You give up, these two are never going to resolve their differences, especially since Jay is acting as if there's no problem.

C. You wait to see if Jay does get the work to Lydia on time. If so, then there's no problem. If not, then you'll address it with Jay at that time.

D. Put Jay on a strict timetable for the work to be done. Ask Lydia to give you a status report as to whether or not she got it.

E. Any combination of the above or another option entirely.

Tools you might use:

SOLUTIONS AND TOOLS: Bad Behavior

Body Odor

Best option: B

When someone comes to you with a complaint about someone else's behavior, it's always best to take a neutral position until you can get the facts about what happened. Locate Cassie as soon as you can and ask her whether the incident took place. If she asks if Abdul complained, tell her that's irrelevant. If she denies the incident occurred, you may have to ask HR or another manager to conduct a detailed investigation. If she admits the incident occurred, then use the Manager's Straight Talk tool.

Next best option: C

Although we believe the incident is serious enough to require you giving Cassie a "Manager's Straight Talk," you may feel the behavior does not warrant private discussions with Cassie's, and Brian's manager. That's your choice. But reminding your team about treating others with respect will probably not hurt and may help.

Tools to Use: "Manager's Straight Talk" (page 79).

Burnout

Best option: B and C in combination

You are in a very tough spot here because this problem has many facets. First, if Keith is having an affair with a junior staff member, which is clearly against policy, it has to stop; however, you should not investigate unless you are trained to do so. Calling in HR or an outside authority to do an investigation will protect you in the event of a lawsuit. Secondly, Keith's performance has clearly suffered as a result of his personal issues. You can't just ignore this because you will risk things becoming worse for Keith, you, the clients, and the staff. Shifting some of the work away from Keith is a good short-term solution; however, it won't do in the long run because people won't understand the complexity of it and may begin resenting you or Keith. So, ensuring that Keith gets some counseling and/or therapy for his personal issues is important to bringing his overall performance back in line. You can ask HR to identify resources, or you can look into some and advise him of them yourself.

Tools to Use: A combination of "Coaching your Colleague," (page 75) and "Transition Coaching," (page 82). Recommend to Keith that he use "The Changed Man" Technique (page 70).

Customer Service

Best option: B and E in combination

Although you may be comfortable with the level of informality, there are others in the group who may not be. Sooner or later, the atmosphere could rise to a level that could be considered hostile work environment and then you will have some serious problems to deal with. At this point getting everyone together to talk about the issue in a nonthreatening way will be useful. It will also give you an opportunity to remind folks about inappropriate behavior and its impact on others who may not appreciate it. Use the Chippendales calendar as an example and ask that it be removed.

Tools to use: "Manager's Straight Talk" (page 79).

Strained Relations

Best option: A

This is the right option, but it's not going to be easy. You need to let Jay know that you see problems, even if he denies they exist. And you need Lydia to understand that she needs to keep her opinions of others to herself and treat her teammates with respect.

Tools to use: "The 60-Minute Mediation," (page 69) and "Classic Straight Talk," (page 74).

CASE STUDIES: People Problems

Wasted Effort

Role. You are a government employee in a large agency. You are a member of a "tiger team" put together by Stella, a deputy regional administrator within the agency. Stella is in charge of the entire region.

Background. Stella, who has been on the job 12 years, formed the tiger team three months ago to assess training needs in the regional office and to figure out how to allocate the training budget equitably. After working hard for three months your group turned in very well written and carefully thought out report to Stella, expecting her to respond at your next team meeting in one week.

Current Problem. Just before the one-week mark, the meeting got postponed and the Stella went on a one-week off-site meeting in Washington DC. Upon her return a member of the team asked about the report. She replied, "I saw the email before I left but hadn't had the chance to open it. Let's meet next week and I will have an answer by then." It is now the next week and you're in the meeting. After prompting from one of you, Stella announces that things have changed, the internal training budget was cut during the off-site meeting and there is no more money for training; she says, "Let's move on." This is clearly a shock to you and the others on the team. What do you do?

A.   Blow your stack and let her know in no uncertain terms how angry you and the team are about this.

B.   Shrug your shoulders. This is the federal government and things like this happen all the time.

C.   Ask if she's open to hearing how upset you and some of the others on the team are right now. If she is, try to stay calm and let her know how you feel. If she isn't open to it now, ask for an appointment to meet with her about it specifically.

D.   Get up, walk out and call your union rep.

E.   Any combination of the above or another option entirely.

Tools you might use:

Old vs. New

This is based on my experience with Tom and Richard in New York City, outlined in the primer "Diversity Justified."

Role. You are a senior manager in a financial services company.

Background. Richard DeAngelo, SVP of Product Management (white male, late 50's), is a career man with the organization, having worked his way up from the mailroom over 25 years ago. He has been honored with performance awards three times and is considered one of the top leaders in the organization. His record is impeccable and his contacts with major clients and vendors are second to none. He's still going strong and has indicated to one and all that he wants to keep going, as he jokingly says, "Until I drop dead on the job."

Current Problem. There have been recent and rapid changes in your industry that are requiring a large amount of restructuring and reorganization. Most importantly, your company has merged with another and is actively engaged in developing new products and services and marketing them over the Internet and other media. You are responsible for putting together a working group/team who will develop and shepherd these new products and services using new technology. Given Richard's vast experience and knowledge, he would be one of the first you would tap for this project, but Richard is a classic "lone ranger" who works on his own and dominates meetings with his personality. And he openly acknowledges he knows nothing about technology – he doesn't even know how to type! – and feels he is too old to learn new tricks. He's mentioned to you that he's met some of the new "young turks" in the tech group as he calls them, and is certain they feel he has nothing to offer. You suspect he considers you a "young turk" too even though you've got plenty of experience. What do you do?

A.   Confront Richard and tell him to "get over it." Offer him training and other resources to help him come up to speed with the others on the team.

B.   Go over Richard's head to another leader he's comfortable with and get him/her to talk Richard into being involved.

C.   Call a group meeting with everyone you're thinking of putting on this team, including Richard, and learn about each other's unique skills, talents and expertise. Ask the team to generate solutions for leveraging everything that each person brings to the group. Set measurable goals and expectations and be alert to subtle signs of bias such as remarks or excuses about "old-timers" or "geeks" or "cultural differences."

D.   Forget about putting Richard on the group, he'll only disrupt the process.

E.   Offer Richard a combination of personal incentives, making it impossible for him to say no.

F.   Any combination of the above or another option entirely.

Tools you might use:

Pat and her Mom

Role. You are a director of an information technology (IT) group in a large corporation.

Background. Pat is a junior systems analyst in the IT group who has been with the company for approximately five years. She reports to Brad Milford, a new hire, who reports to you. She is Jamaican born and raised but has lived in the US for many years with her mother. She still has a strong accent. Her record is exemplary and she is recognized as one of the top performers in the department and also one of the most professional people to work with. No one has anything negative to say about Pat, except that perhaps she is a bit too "uptight," that she keeps her personal and professional life very separate.

Current Problem. Recently you learned through the grapevine that Pat's mother has Alzheimer's disease and that Linda, a senior analyst who works with her every day, has been covering for Pat occasionally while Pat has taken her mother to the doctor. Brad Milford has said nothing to you about this. Normally, given Pat's past performance and sense of professionalism, you would not be concerned, but you are also aware that primary caregivers for people with Alzheimer's need to devote more and more of their own time to taking care of their loved one as the disease progresses. And your division is undergoing rapid change and growth with more and more requests and burdens being placed upon your group every day. You value Pat's skill, experience and professionalism and you're sure she would be a great manager. And you've been thinking of fast-tracking Pat into a management position in order to help manage this growth. But now you're having second thoughts. What should you do?

A.   Nothing, wait for the problem to surface on its own. Even mentioning to Pat that you know about her mom's illness could get you into hot water legally.

B.   Take Pat off the fasttrack to management; start looking for someone new to go into that slot.

C.   Privately offer Pat your support in regard to her mom's illness. Indicate your willingness to be flexible and creative in finding ways for Pat to continue to be one of your top performers. Have her consider job-sharing, flexi-time and other options that she may not be thinking of. Set goals and expectations with her and monitor them.

D.   Take Brad aside, tell him what you know and suggest he find a way to handle it so the organization is not put at risk.

E.   Meet with Brad and Pat. Discuss your plans for the future of the division and how you see them fitting into it. Wait for them to bring up their concerns. If nothing surfaces, move forward with your plans.

F.   Any combination of the above or another option entirely.

Tools you might use:

Personality Clash or Gender Bias?

Role. You are a manager of an administrative department.

Background. John and Sue are coworkers in your department and occasionally have projects that they both work on and meetings that they attend together. Recently one of Sue's colleagues came to you and reported the following:

Current Problem. It seems that Sue doesn't mind working on projects with John but has noticed that she seems to be less patient in her dealings with John. When she gets together with John to discuss a project, she doesn't feel that she gets a chance to talk about her own ideas or to share her own perspective. She feels her input is minimized and often ignored. She knows that John is smart and has a lot to share, but she perceives John as being very self-absorbed and incapable of understanding or respecting her values and ideas. This has even extended into personal conversations. The way Sue sees it, John just likes to hear himself talk. It has become so bad that Sue has gone out of her way to exclude John from coworker conversations. She intentionally walks around his office to avoid any conversation except what is business related. She finds herself talking with her coworkers about the situation but is afraid to deal with the situation directly. She knows that she will not be with this department much longer and therefore will not have to deal with John much more. As a result, she does not feel compelled to talk with John about his behavior. Now that you know all of these things, what should you do?

A.   Nothing. Sue's about to go. This will all be moot when she's gone.

B.   Get Sue and John together and lay it all out on the table. Make them work out their differences.

C.   Speak with Sue in private and see if what her colleague has said is accurate. Let Sue take the lead on what she wants to do.

D.   Speak with John in private and let him know that he has to change his attitude and behavior, giving him clear guidelines as to how he should improve and setting a timetable for when it all has to happen.

E.   Tell the colleague to mind his/her own business.

F.   Gather everyone together to discuss relationships, perhaps hold a team development workshop or a diversity seminar.

G.   Any combination of the above.

Tools you might use:

SOLUTIONS AND TOOLS: People Problems

Wasted Effort

Best Option: C

It's vital that you let Stella know that you and the team put a lot of time and effort in on the report and that at the very least she should acknowledge this. Stella needs to know that communicating with you or another member of the team, as soon as she found out the budget had been cut, would have been an easier "let down" than being told during a meeting two weeks later.

Tools to Use: "Classic Straight Talk," (page 74) and "The 2-Minute Redirect," (page 68).

Old vs. New

Best Options: A, C and E

Richard needs to be acknowledged, but he also needs to work with the others and provide his expertise. You have to play "good cop" and "bad cop" with Richard at the same time. You might want to offer him some incentives, but that could backfire. And you have to ensure the others on the team see his value and leverage what he knows.

Tools to Use: "Coaching Your Colleague," (page 75) and "Transition Coaching," (page 82).

Pat and her Mom

Best Option: "F," a combination of A and E.

Although it's likely you really want to let Pat know that you are willing to help her with her personal situation, if you do so before she tells you about it, you could get yourself in legal hot water, especially if you have to terminate her sometime in the future. She could sue you for wrongful termination. So, you should not let her know that you are aware of her mother's illness. But, you must let her know that you value her and her work and that you want to see her succeed. Tell her about your plans to promote her and Give her the opportunity to let you know about her mother's situation. If she does, document that she did so.

Tools to Use: "Transition Coaching," (page 82) and "Coaching Your Colleague," (page 75).

Personalities Clashes or Gender Bias?

Best Option: D and F

While it's always helpful to do some team building and diversity work, letting John know that he needs to find new ways of interacting with others is equally important. Don't just assume the problem will go away when Sue leaves. Part of your job as a manager is to find ways for people to get along and work together better. Part of John's job should be to be aware of his personal style and how it impacts others. Your job is to let him know and keep him on track toward developing himself.

Tools to Use: A modified "Classic Straight Talk," (page 74) and "Coaching Your Colleague," (page 75).

CASE STUDIES: Sticky Situations

The Anonymous Message

Role. You are a line manager to whom a number of engineers report.

Background. Andre Kavetz, a Russian/Israeli, is one of your newest team members. He is a good worker although a little bit negative about life in general. You assume that is just part of his Russian character. There have been no problems with him at all since he has been with your company.

Current Problem. A few minutes ago, you got a call from Andre. He seemed really upset and asked if he could come to your office to talk with you. You say "sure." When he arrives, Andre hands you a printout of an anonymous e-mail that he received: *"Everyone knows you Russians cheat in college. They ought to send you back to Siberia where you belong."* What do you do?

A.   Tell Andre to calm down and not to worry about it, it's just a stupid prank.

B.   Tell Andre to go to HR or legal immediately and report it.

C.   Use the H.E.A.R. technique, take the email and report the incident to HR or legal

D.   Use the H.E.A.R. technique and immediately start trying to track down the person who did it.

E.   Take the email, tell Andre to go back to work and report it to HR or legal yourself.

F.   Ask Andre if he knows who might have sent it and ask if other things like this have happened to him.

G.   Any combination of the above.

Tools you might use:

Brad vs. Linda

Role. You are the new chief technology officer of information technology (IT) for a fast growing financial services firm.

Background. The moment you arrived three weeks ago, you realize the demands on the IT group are growing every day and you need to bring on board more people – technical folks and IT managers – as soon as possible.

So you had a discussion with your boss, the CIO, who approved your idea to create the post of director of IT. He suggested that since being a manager requires more than technical knowledge/skills, that you make an MBA a requirement for the job. You then asked the recruiters to come up with a short list of potential candidates.

Current Problem. After looking at the files of current employees, you identify Linda Espinoza as being potentially right for this job due to her length of service (15 years!) and high level of technical training, knowledge and skills. However, after looking more closely through her file, you realized she has no MBA, and after speaking with the CIO again, you found out that Linda's personal style is considered "very abrasive" by him and a number of people who have worked with her. Also, one person with whom you spoke acknowledged that Linda "practically built the IT department single-handedly." However, he used the "b-word" in reference to her personality. And you heard a rumor that a former employee in Linda's department left the company because he could not work with her.

Meanwhile the recruiters have identified some potential candidates, including a 25-year-old white male named Brad Milford, who is a recent graduate from Stanford University's MBA program. Given the scarcity of IT people and even greater scarcity of IT people with Stanford MBA's, you immediately decided to interview him first, to get a gut reaction as to whether he would be right for the job.

You also speak with Linda Espinoza who indicates that she is well aware she is the "right person for the job." It becomes clear that there's no question Linda is technically competent, and in terms of her experience and ability to manage complex technical projects and problems, you have few worries there either. It's her people skills that concern you. During your meeting with Linda she was very professional, but also very cold and distant. She seemed to have a huge chip on her shoulder about the organization in general. She also said her work style was "terse" and that some people don't know how to take her.

The first interview with Brad went extremely well. And after informing the CIO, you call Brad in for a second interview. At the end of the interview with

Brad, which went fairly well, your boss, the CIO, took you aside and encouraged you to hire Brad as soon as possible. He suggested that given the rapid growth of the company, "something that better suits Linda's personal style is bound to open up very soon." The CIO seemed to feel very strongly about it, but you're concerned about Brad's lack of experience and you're certain Linda would take the promotion if you offered it to her. What do you do?

A. Since the posting calls for an MBA and Linda does not have one, your decision is easy: hire Brad. Give Linda a fat bonus to keep her happy, promise to put her into the next IT management slot that opens up.

B. Promote Linda after a frank discussion with her in which you raise your concerns about her people skills. Set clear goals and expectations for her and establish a timeline for her. Recommend and offer to pay for "People Skills for Managers" training for her. Bring Brad in under her in a new position, assistant director of IT, if he'll take it. Inform the CIO of your decision and gauge his response. Monitor Brad's and Linda's performance closely.

C. Since the posting calls for an MBA, hire Brad into the director of IT slot and create a new position for Linda, assistant director of IT, reporting to Brad. Inform him of Linda's personal style and request that he monitor Linda closely. Recommend to Linda that she get an MBA.

D. Keep looking for someone with an MBA and more experience than Brad.

E. Any combination of the above or another option entirely.

Tools you might use:

Changes on the Line

Role. You are a brand-new supervisor in a manufacturing division of a fast-growing/changing telecommunications equipment company. You oversee approximately 15 employees on a specific assembly line. All of these employees are male and Vietnamese, and many of them are related to each other. You are not Vietnamese and you do not speak their language at all. Only a few of the Vietnamese can speak English.

Background. When you were assigned the job of supervising this group, management warned you that this group believes it "owns" this specific line and does not respond well to authority or requests from management for flexibility on hours and output. In addition you've been told the group does not listen to the repair technicians or maintenance workers who service the equipment on this line. Still, this group works very hard and never complains; they keep to themselves, keep their heads down and generally do a good job.

When assigned this job, you were informed by management that the entire line, along with many others, needs to be retooled and upgraded in order to meet new specifications requested by your company's clients. This will mean shutting down the line for a period, as well as some significant changes in the way the line operates and serves the rest of the manufacturing division. You don't know the full extent of the changes, nor how it will affect the makeup or role of this group, but you are certain that new people, non-Vietnamese with other skills/knowledge, will need to be added to the group. Also you are sure some of the other lines may want to pull employees from your line into theirs. In short there are going to be a lot of changes coming very soon, but as always happens, you're not sure what all the changes will be nor when they will take place.

Current Problem. You've been told that your performance evaluation will be based on how smoothly and efficiently these changes occur. And you personally committed to management that you would do this with the least upset to the productivity of the line, to you and the people on the line. However, management has told you this would be a "perfect opportunity to dismantle the little Vietnam" that this line has become. How are you going to accomplish this, and the upcoming changes and do it all with the least amount of cost, upset and trouble to the company and everyone involved?

A.   Wait until the very last moment before the first change has to happen, and then call all the employees on the line together and tell them: "everything is about to change, cooperate, get used to it, and you'll do fine. Fight the changes and you will not be working with us anymore." Wait to see who cooperates and who doesn't and then change the makeup of the group based on those observations.

B.   Find out who within the group has the best understanding of English and who has the most authority/respect from the others, and pull that person in for a private meeting. Tell him to get the others ready for big changes and that you want him to keep the others in line. If anyone causes any problems, you will hold him accountable. If it all goes smoothly, he will be rewarded in some way to be determined later.

C.   Go to the group as soon as you can and let them know there will be big changes coming soon and what they might look like and how they might happen. Tell them that this is their opportunity to have a say in how the changes are going to be made. Solicit their suggestions either as a whole group or ask them to meet in small groups to make suggestions as to how the changes can best be made with the least amount of trouble. Let them know that you will listen closely to all of their suggestions, but that you have final say in what happens. Add that you will try to be as fair as you can under the circumstances. Follow this process and continue to communicate with them as the entire change process goes forward. Evaluate the process and adjust as you go.

D.   Come up with a game plan, schedule and strategy for making all the changes and then execute the changes as quietly and quickly as you can, telling only those who need to know as you go along. Keep them guessing as to what is going to happen next and do not respond to any requests for information. Sympathize greatly with anyone who complains or has a problem, but tell them it's "out of my control" and that you're just doing what you've been told to do by senior management.

E.   Put your résumé out on the net, there's no way you are going to win in this situation.

F.   Any combination of the above or another option entirely.

Tools you might use:

The New Customer

Role. You are a manager of a field office in California, selling commercial real estate with a team of eight brokers, all of whom are white, two of whom are female.

Background. The team is supported by a staff of four: a male African-American named Michael Murray, a female Asian-American and two white women. To recruit Michael onto staff, you promised to support him in his desire to become a broker. He is meeting every one of the requirements to become a broker in a very careful and determined manner and he's just about ready to become one. This is just as you'd hoped and expected.

Current Problem. The office is thriving; you're getting a lot of business through referrals. In fact the current brokers are swamped with work and you're getting more work every day. A week ago you received a "heads-up" call from a very good client of yours, who is referring a close friend of his, the COO of a new high-tech company. Your client indicated that although this friend's business is high-tech manufacturing, its leadership is made up of older white males who are "conservative in the Southern tradition." They are maintaining their assembly locations in the South, but they are looking to move their corporate headquarters of about 50-75 people to southern California, and your client is certain you and your team will serve them well. This is not a huge account by any means, but it is an account that you'd rather not see your competitors serve, and you want to keep your friend happy too. What do you do?

A.   Call Michael in and tell him, "This is your first account, don't screw it up." Then watch him like a hawk.

B.   Give the potential client to one of your experienced white male brokers. That should secure a deal for you, make your team money and keep your friend happy.

C.   Tell Michael he's on this account, but only as a junior partner to one of your experienced brokers. Michael will receive only a percentage of the commission. Promise him he'll get the full commission on the next deal.

D.   Tell your friend that you're too busy, but you'll find another local real estate team to handle the job.

E.   Any combination of the above or another option entirely.

Tools you might use:

Off The Wagon

Role. You are a manager of a team of 20 government employees, with support from outside contractors.

Background. A few months ago you contracted with an employment agency for the services of an administrative assistant. They assigned Ian, an ex-marine who impressed you with his experience, skills and his no-nonsense approach. On his first day Ian informed you that he is an alcoholic, regularly attended. AA and hadn't had a drink for nearly a year. He assured you that this would not impact his work. He said his agency was aware of this. For the next few months things went well. Ian tended to have a short fuse and was very intense about everything, but his work was exemplary and always delivered on time.

Current Problem. A few days ago Ian informed you that his ex-wife was moving out of town that evening. He asked for the afternoon off to close out some business arrangements with her. You granted his request. The next morning you expected to see Ian at his desk, but he did not come in. You called his home, but there was no answer, so you left a message. He did not come in the next day either. Concerned, you contacted his agency. They had not heard from him, nor could they locate him by phone. Ian finally appeared this morning, more than an hour after his normal time. He looked awful, as if he hadn't slept in days. You called him into your office and closed the door. He seemed very tense and nervous and he closed the blinds before sitting down. Then he immediately burst into tears, saying he had fallen off the wagon after hearing that his ex-wife had decided to marry her new boyfriend. Between sobs, Ian said how sorry he was, how he felt he had let you down and how angry he was at himself. Suddenly he reached down to his sock, searching for something. For a second that seemed to last an hour, you thought he might pull out a gun. Instead he pulled out a tiny bottle of vodka and downed it in one gulp. What do you do?

A. Get up and leave the room as fast as you can, telling Ian you'll be right back. Call the police.

B. Tell Ian to take a few deep breaths to calm himself. Reassure him that everything will work out and that you can and are willing to help him. Ask him if there is anyone you can call for him, a friend or family member, who is aware of his condition and can assist him. Once he appears calmer, tell him you'd like to open the door and then work with him on next steps.

C. Tell him to go to his desk and collect his belongings. Call for help to escort him off the premises.

D. Tell Ian to stay put for a moment and that you need to get some air to think about what to do. Get up slowly, open the door and go for help.

E. Any combination of the above or another option entirely.

Tools you might use:

SOLUTIONS AND TOOLS: Sticky Situations

The Anonymous Message

Best Option: C and F

Andre needs help calming down; the H.E.A.R. technique will do this. In addition you need to report the incident to HR or legal. This could be part of a pattern of behavior here that may rise to the level of a hostile work environment. Under the law, the employer (including you – Andre's manager) has a responsibility to provide a work environment that is free of harassing and/or intimidating behavior. Unless you have the training, time and ability to conduct a thorough investigation, this is best left to HR or legal. Nevertheless you need to reassure Andre that you consider this a serious issue and you will address it accordingly.

Tools to Use: "H.E.A.R," (page 78).

Brad vs. Linda

Best Option: B

Most of us shy away from conflict and people with a personal style that is considered by most to be abrasive. But our inability to manage an abrasive person is our problem, not theirs. As managers we have to find ways of developing everyone on our team– this means leveraging their skills and experience. Avoiding Linda and not promoting her would be the worst thing we could do, because if you do, she'll probably leave and take all of that knowledge and skill with her, possibly to your competitor. But promoting her without making it clear that she needs to adjust her personal style would be an equal disaster. There's nothing wrong with making her promotion conditional.

Tools to Use: A modified "Manager's Straight Talk," (page 79) replacing the steps involving the company's policy and procedures with a very clear list of expectations about her behavior. Establish a schedule of quarterly meetings to assess her progress.

Changes on the Line

Best Option: C

This is one of those tough situations where you have to work hard to reach out to people who are very different from you. Sure, you could go with option D and force the changes without consulting the workers, but this will no doubt backfire on you and probably cause a lot more harm than good. No, the best thing to do is be open and honest with them, treat them with respect and listen to what they have to say. This will take time and patience, but in the end you will find you have earned their respect and cooperation.

Tools to Use: Modified "H.E.A.R," (page 78), modified "Transition Coaching," (page 82).

The New Customer

Best Option: C
Although it might seem as if money is the most important thing in real estate, honoring your commitments and doing the right thing by your staff is just as important. In this case, giving the new client to Michael with supervision by a senior partner is the right thing to do and it will pay off well for everyone if the senior partner you ask Michael to work with is sensitive and a good mentor. Caving in to racist perceptions and stereotypes is the wrong thing to do.

Tools to Use: Modified "2-Minute Redirect," (page 68); "Verbal Agreement Contract," (page 83); and "F.A.C.T.," (page 20).

Off The Wagon

Best Option: B
Although instinctually you may be tempted to try to run out of there and get away from Ian immediately, trying to do so may backfire. Any sudden action on your part might upset Ian even more. He could become violent in some manner or refuse to let you out. By speaking calmly with him and by letting him know you are willing to help him, it's likely that Ian will stay calmer. Nevertheless your safety and comfort are important too. Open the door as soon as you can, tell Ian you're not going anywhere, and stand in it as you talk with him. If you're comfortable doing so, continue working with him to devise a plan of action that he is going to take for the next few hours so that at the end of the discussion, he will walk out your door on his own. Immediately notify the proper authorities in your organization and his supervisor at his firm.

Tools to Use: "Coaching Your Colleague," (page 75).

INDEX by Behaviors, Problems and Situations
(with recommended tools and reading)

Bad Behavior –
Note: For each of the following behaviors, contact HR/legal before (if possible) taking action. After a complete investigation, if it is determined that the misconduct warrants termination, we recommend you use "The Termination Meeting" (page 81).

Adultery- see (Affairs)
Affairs- use "Manager's Straight Talk" page 79, "Coaching your Colleague" page 75.
Alcoholism- see (Substance), read "Off The Wagon" page 107.
Arson- contact security/police
Bribery- use "Classic Straight Talk," page 74, report immediately.
Clothing- see (Offensive Clothing), read "Where Are We Now?" page 41.
Credit cards
      Inappropriate use- contact legal department/senior management
Decisions- use "Decision Matrix" page 72.
Destruction of property- contact security/police
Discrimination- Report immediately, use "Classic Straight Talk" page
Drugs- see (Substance)
Fraud- contact HR/legal /senior management
Gambling- use "Manager's Straight Talk" page 79.
Harassment
      Sexual- Report immediately, optional use "Classic Straight Talk" page 74.
      Third Party- contact hr/legal in your firm and/or security/police
Hate mail- contact security/police, use "Manager's Straight Talk" page 79.
Inappropriate- see (Offensive)
Obstructing criminal investigations- use "Manager's Straight Talk" page 79.
Offensive
      Cartoons and Photos- use "Manager's Straight Talk" page 79.
      Clothing- use "Classic Straight Talk" page 74.
Language- use "Classic Straight Talk" page 74, or "Manager's Straight Talk" page 79.
      Written/physical gestures- optional use "Classic Straight Talk" page 74.
Pornography
      Websites- use "Manager's Straight Talk" page 79.
      Emails- use "Manager's Straight Talk" page 79.
Relationships
      Strained- use "60-minute Mediation" page 69, "Classic Straight Talk" page 74.
      Sexual- see (Affairs)
Retaliation
      Against people who don't accede to unreasonable requests- use "Manager's Straight Talk" page 79.
Against whistle-blowers- use "Manager's Straight Talk" page 79.
Spying- use "Manager's Straight Talk" page 79.
Substance
      Abuse- use "Manager's Straight Talk" page 79, "Coaching your Colleague" page 75 and "Changed Man Technique" page 70.
      Distribution, dealing- "Manager's Straight Talk" page 79.

Theft
>   Company property/funds- contact legal department/senior management
>   Personal property/funds- contact police, legal department/senior management

Violating city, state and federal employment, environmental, and trade laws- contact
>   police, government agencies, legal department/senior management, use
>   "Manager's Straight Talk" page 79.

Violence- use "H E A R" page 78, "60-minute Mediation" page 69 and
>   "Classic Straight Talk" page 74.

Voyeurism- see (Spying)

People Problems –

It's always a good idea to contact HR /legal or senior management before taking action.

Absenteeism/lateness- use "Sandwich" page 80, "2-minute Redirect" page 68.

Adultry- see (Affairs)

Affairs- use "Manager's Straight Talk" page 79, "Coaching your Colleague" page 75,
read "Harassment in a Nutshell" page 39.

Decisions- use "Decision Matrix" page 72.

Discrimination- Report immediately to HR/legal and senior management, use
>   "Manager's Straight Talk" page 79.

Exclusive/prejudicial behaviors, clubs, committees and teams- use "End State
>   Statement" page 77, "Classic Straight Talk" page 74.

Falsifying reports, documents, time cards- use "Manager's Straight Talk" page 79.

Favoritism- use "The End State Statement" page 77, "2-minute Redirect" page 68.

Fighting- see (Violence)

Fraternization with subordinates, excessively- use "Classic Straight Talk" page 74.

Gossip- use "Classic Straight talk" page 74, "The Sandwich Technique" page 80, "Verbal
>   Agreement Contract" page 83.

Ignoring safety rules and regulations- use "Classic Straight Talk" page 74.

Illness- see (Medical Problems)

Inappropriate- see (Offensive)

Industrial espionage- see (Spying)

Lying- use "Classic Straight talk" page 74.

Medical Problems- use "Coaching your Colleague" page 75,
>   "Transition Coaching" page 82.

Negative team activities- use "Manager's Straight Talk" page 79,
>   "End State Statement" page 77.

Offensive
>   Cartoons and Photos- use "Classic Straight Talk" page 74.
>   Clothing- use "Classic Straight Talk" page 74.

Language- use "Classic Straight Talk" page 74 or "Manager's Straight Talk" page 79.
>   Written/physical gestures- optional use "Classic Straight Talk" page 74

Personal use of company computer and equipment- use "Classic Straight Talk" page 74.

Personalities
>   Aggressive- use "Coaching your Colleague" page, "H E A R" page 78, "Verbal
>   Agreement Contract" page 83, read pages 12-14.

Sticky Situations

Drugs- see (Substance)

Illness- see (Medical Problems)

Inappropriate- see (Offensive)

Medical Problems- use "Coaching your Colleague" page 75,
> "Transition Coaching" page 82, read "Pat And Her Mom" pages 96, 99.

Mistakes, errors and omissions- "2-minute Redirect" page 68,
> "The Sandwich Technique" page 80, read "Trust" pages 22-24.

Miscommunications, misunderstandings- use "Verbal Agreement Contract" page 83.

Offensive
> Cartoons and Photos- optional use "Classic Straight Talk" page 74.
> Clothing- use "Classic Straight Talk" page 74.

Language- use "Classic Straight Talk" page 74 or "Manager's Straight Talk" page 79.
> Written/physical gestures- optional use "Classic Straight Talk" page 74.

Personalities
> Challenging, aggressive attitudes- use "Coaching your Colleague" page 75.
> Depression- use "Coaching your Colleague" page 75,
>> "Changed Man Technique" page 70.

Promotions- use "Decision Matrix" page 72.

Relationships
> Strained- use "60-minute mediation" page 69, optional "Coaching
>> your Colleague" page 75.

Sexual- see (Affairs)

Requests
> by employees/customers for preferential treatment- use "Decision Matrix" page 72.
> for time off- use "Decision Matrix" page 72.
> for overly-flexible arrangements- use "The Flexibility Gauge" page 19.
> for transfer, salary increase, bonus or leave of absence- use
>> "Decision Matrix" page 72.
> by employees/customers for discounts/ free goods and/or services- use
>> "Decision Matrix" page 72.

by customers for service from particular employees- use "Decision Matrix" page 72.

Sociopath behavior- use "Coaching your Colleague" page 75,
> "Changed Man Technique" page 70.

Stupid, inane, degrading remarks- use "Classic Straight Talk" page 74,
> "The Sandwich Technique" page 80, "Coaching your Colleague" page 75.

Subversive behaviors- use "Coaching your Colleague" page 75.

Substance
> Abuse- contact HR/legal, use "Coaching your Colleague" page 75 and
>> "Changed Man Technique" page 70.
> Distribution, dealing- contact HR/legal, "Manager's Straight Talk" page 79.

Transitions- use "Transition Coaching" page 82, "H E A R" page 78.

Unethical business practices- use "Coaching your Colleague" page 75.

Verbal
> Challenging, aggressive comments- use "Classic Straight Talk" page 74.
> Stupid, inane comments- use "Classic Straight Talk" page 74.

Resources, References, Chapter Notes

Bucher, Richard D. *Diversity Consciousness.* Upper Saddle River, NJ: Prentince Hall, 2000.

Carr-Ruffino, Norma. *Diversity Success Strategies.* Woburn, MA: Butterworth-Heinemann, 1999.

Clark, Don. "Training Statistics & Benchmarking." 29 Apr. 2001. Northwest Link website. 1 May 2001 <http://www.nwlink.com/~donclark/hrd/trainsta.html>.

Consortium for Research on Emotional Intelligence in Organization. 2002. www.eiconsortium.org

Covey, Stephen. R. *First Things First.* New York: Fireside, 1995.

De Pree, Max. *Leadership is an Art.* New York: Dell Publishing, 1989.

DiversityInc.com. 2 May 2002. DiversityInc.com. <http://www.diversityinc.com/>.

Dotlich, David L. and Noel, James L. *Action Learning.* San Francisco: Jossey-Bass, 1998.

Doyle, Michael and Straus, David. *How to make Meetings Work.* New York: Jove, 1982.

EEOC. 24 April 2002. U.S. Equal Employment Opportunity Commission. < http://www.eeoc.gov/>.

Fisher, Roger and Ury, William. *Getting to Yes.* New York: Penguin Books, 1991.

Goffee, Rob and Jones, Gareth. *The Character of a Corporation.* New York: HarperCollins, 1998.

Goleman, Daniel. *Emotional Intelligence.* New York: Bantam Books, 1997.

_____. *Working with Emotional Intelligence.* New York: Bantam Books, 1998.

Grensing-Pophal, Lin. *The HR Book.* Bellingham, WA: Self-Counsel Press, 2000.

Louis Harris & Associates. Poll of 782 workers: March 28, 1994.

Lussier, Robert N. *Human Relations in Organizations.* Chicago: Irwin, 1996.

Miles, Robert H. *Leading Corporate Transformation.* San Francisco: Jossey-Bass, 1997.

Moore, J. I. *Writers on Strategy and Strategic Management.* New York: Penguin Books, 1992.

Morrison, Ann M. *The New Leaders.* San Francisco: Jossey-Bass, 1996.

Roberts, Wess and Ross, Bill. *Make it So.* New York: Pocket Books, 1995.

Statistical Abstract, The. 4 Apr. 2002. US Census Bureau. 6 May 2002 <http://www.census.gov/statab/www/part3.html#employ>

Thandeka. *Learning to be White.* New York: Continuum Publishing Group, 1999.

Thomas, Roosevelt R. *Building a House for Diversity.* New York: Amacon, 1999.

Weisinger, Hendrie D. et al. *Emotional Intelligence at Work.* San Francisco: Jossey-Bass, 1997.

List of Key Concepts and Best Practices

About the Author

Gregg Ward is a thought leader, speaker, author, consultant, trainer, executive coach, and entrepreneurial business owner. For over 25 years Gregg's focus has been on respect and respectful leadership, and the powerful and measureable benefits that they bring to leaders and their organizations.

As Chief Executive Officer of the Gregg Ward Group, Gregg's extensive client list includes ADP, Booz Allen Hamilton, Bristol-Myers Squibb, Burger King, Ford Motor Company, Harley-Davidson, Intercontinental Hotels Group, Kaiser Permanente, Merck Medco, Qualcomm, the US Navy and Warner Bros Studios, among many others.

Gregg began his work in the mid-1980's as a specialist trainer for the New York City Police Department. Since then he has developed and delivered over 2,000 separate keynote speeches, programs and seminars; facilitated scores of strategic planning sessions and offsite meetings; written numerous books and articles; and coached hundreds of senior executives and managers throughout North America and Western Europe.

In addition to this book, Gregg's publications include articles and opinion pieces in national and international publications and trade journals, and the forthcoming books "The Respectful Leader: a little story about a big idea for your business," and "The Dog Who Walked Backwards: managing yourself to success." Gregg is also a frequent guest commentator on radio, television and in print, most recently in The Wall Street Journal, The Street and on Fox News.

Gregg is a Board Certified Coach (BCC) and held the Certified Management Consultant (CMC) credential for over 10 years. He holds a BFA from Boston University and is certified in the leadership assessments FIRO-Business, Workplace Big-5, DISC and The Leadership 360. Formerly an adjunct professor at San Diego State University and Cal State San Marcos, Gregg is currently an Adjunct Coach with The Center for Creative Leadership.

The Gregg Ward Group is headquartered in San Diego and has offices in New York, Miami, The Bay Area, Atlanta, and London.

Contact - Gregg Ward Group 619-461-6777
inquire@greggwardgroup.com

For more information, please visit our website:
GreggWardGroup.com

CPSIA information can be obtained
at www.ICGtesting.com
Printed in the USA
FSOW01n1227221015
12467FS